UNITED ARAB EMIRATES

MODERN NATIONS —OF THE— WORLD

BY DEBRA A. MILLER

LUCENT BOOKS

An imprint of Thomson Gale, a part of The Thomson Corporation

THOMSON

GALE™

Detroit • New York • San Francisco • San Diego • New Haven, Conn.
Waterville, Maine • London • Munich

TITLES IN THE MODERN NATIONS OF THE WORLD SERIES INCLUDE:

For more information, contact
Lucent Books
27500 Drake Rd.
Farmington Hills, MI 48331-3535
Or you can visit our Internet site at http://www.gale.com

LIBRARY OF CONGRESS CATALOGING-IN-PUBLICATION DATA

Miller, Debra A.
  United Arab Emirates / by Debra A. Miller.
    p. cm. -- (Modern nations of the world)
  Includes bibliographical references and index.
  Contents: Hidden riches—The journey to prosperity—Unity and progress—Tradition, religion, and culture—Life in the modern UAE—Challenges ahead.
    ISBN 1-59018-627-3 (hardcover : alk. paper)
    1. United Arab Emirates--Juvenile literature. I. Title. II. Series.
DS247.T8M55 2004
953.57—dc22
                                                        2004011868

CONTENTS

INTRODUCTION

AN OASIS OF STABILITY

The United Arab Emirates (UAE) is a small nation located in the southern Persian Gulf near Saudi Arabia. The United Arab Emirates is a relatively young country, coming into existence in 1971. Despite its youth and diminutive size, the UAE is a major oil exporter and an oasis of stability in a region most often associated in the popular imagination with revolution and unrest. The UAE is also one of the United States' strongest Arab allies.

The level of prosperity in the UAE is remarkable even in a region where petroleum has made many nations wealthy. The UAE developed into a technologically advanced nation faster than some of its neighbors, even some whose oil industries developed decades earlier. Today, it is one of the richest countries in the world and the second-wealthiest Arab nation; among oil-producing countries in the Middle East, only Qatar is wealthier. The UAE's per capita income (the country's total income divided by its population) is close to twenty thousand dollars per year, similar to that of other developed countries such as the United States, Great Britain, and Germany.

The UAE also stands out as one of the Middle East's most stable countries. Contrary to many predictions and despite occasional squabbles among its seven component emirates, the UAE has maintained its unity in a system of government called a federation. And unlike some other Middle East nations, it has not experienced significant social unrest, political terrorism, or violent crime. Many have attributed this stability to the leadership skills of the UAE's president, Sheikh Zayed bin Sultan al-Nuhayyan.

Even more surprising in the minds of observers, the UAE absorbed the dramatic changes brought by sudden wealth without losing its essential Arab character. Although isolated collections of huts have largely given way to air-conditioned condos, and camels have been replaced by luxury automobiles, citizens of the UAE have retained many of their traditions and their religion. Many are devout in saying prayers and following Islamic rules of behavior, practice modesty in their dress, and are, above all, loyal to their families, one of the strongest of Arab values.

Yet another component of the UAE's success story is the fact that it has accomplished all this without closing its society to the outside world. Instead, it has remained tolerant of other cultures and religions and employs workers and businesspeople from around the world to help its economy thrive. As a result, the UAE is known as one of the most cosmopolitan and desirable business and tourist destinations in the world. Multinational companies such as Microsoft and FedEx have regional headquarters there. In addition, the UAE is home to first-class hotels and resorts, and is a shopper's paradise, where gold and other luxury items are readily available.

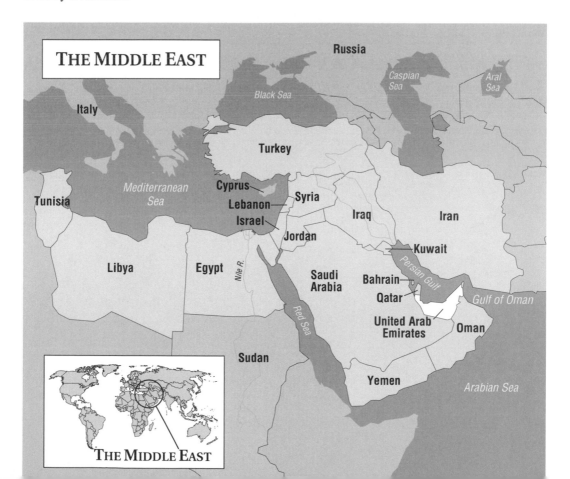

Pictured is the skyline of the coastal city of Dubai in the United Arab Emirates, one of the most politically stable nations in the Middle East.

The UAE is unique in that even as it has opened its doors to the United States and other Western countries such as Britain and France, it has managed to maintain friendly relations with neighboring nations that are not on good terms with the West. It has become a leader among the other states of the southern gulf, helping to form a multistate organization dedicated to joint economic development and defense. The UAE also has avoided open conflict with neighboring states such as Iran, even after that country seized parts of the UAE's territory.

The experiment in tribal unity called the UAE has been, by many measures, a grand success. Although there have been minor setbacks and disputes, its short life as a nation has in most respects set a shining example of leadership and cooperation. If its past is an indicator, the UAE's future can be expected to be bright.

Hidden Riches

The UAE occupies a tiny, crescent-shaped peninsula of land along the southeastern part of the Persian Gulf (also called the Arabian Gulf). It has a gulf coastline that stretches for 430 miles, and a 56-mile coastline along the Gulf of Oman to the east. Landward, the UAE borders on the nations of Qatar (to the northwest), Saudi Arabia (to the southwest), and Oman (to the east). Yet the total area of the UAE is only about 30,000 square miles—a little smaller than the state of Maine. The landmass that comprises the UAE is mostly barren desert that appears to offer little in the way of resources. The country's main riches lie deep under its desert sands and seas.

From Deserts to Mountains

The UAE is made up of seven emirates, or states—Dubai, Abu Dhabi, Sharjah, Ras al-Khaimah, Fujairah, Umm al Qaywayn, and Ajman—which vary widely in size. The emirates are also very different geographically.

The largest of the seven emirates, Abu Dhabi, accounts for 87 percent of the UAE's total area, or about twenty-six thousand square miles, borders the gulf and occupies an area in the western part of the country, next to Saudi Arabia. Abu Dhabi is mostly desert, its land characterized by vast stretches of fine sand starting three to nine miles from the coast and extending to the UAE's border with Saudi Arabia. High winds that blow from the northwest can pile the sand into dunes hundreds of feet high. Almost nothing can live among these dunes. Yet the desert area of Abu Dhabi also has two important oases where wells provide enough water to support settlements. These are the Liwa Oasis, in the

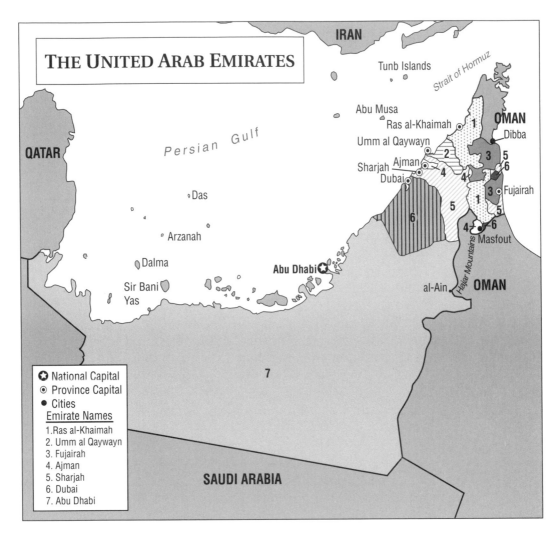

THE UNITED ARAB EMIRATES

IRAN

Tunb Islands

Strait of Hormuz

Abu Musa

Ras al-Khaimah

OMAN

Dibba

Umm al Qaywayn

Persian Gulf

Sharjah Ajman

Dubai

Das

Arzanah

Fujairah

Dalma

Abu Dhabi

al-Ain   OMAN

Hajar Mountains

Masfout

Sir Bani
Yas

7

⊗ National Capital
⊙ Province Capital
● Cities
Emirate Names
1. Ras al-Khaimah
2. Umm al Qaywayn
3. Fujairah
4. Ajman
5. Sharjah
6. Dubai
7. Abu Dhabi

QATAR

SAUDI ARABIA

south near Saudi Arabia, and the Buraimi Oasis, along the
border with Oman. At these sites, there is enough water to
irrigate small farms and groves of date palms.

Nearer the coast, Abu Dhabi is marked by low lands interrupted by many lagoons and estuaries. These bodies of
water range from brackish to as salty as seawater. Most of
the land in this coastal area is covered by salt flats (called
sabkhas), created by evaporation. These areas, with their
thick layer of salt, support no plant life. The *sabkhas* bake in
the hot sun and sometimes the salt crust is so tough that vehicles can be driven on it; periodically, however, high tides
or rain turn the *sabkhas* into impassable swamps.

Given the inhospitality of the terrain, the majority of Abu Dhabi's people live on the dozens of islands that lie just off-shore. Indeed, its capital city and largest population center is located on Abu Dhabi Island, a triangle-shaped island located off the northeastern part of the coast. Another populated island is Dalma, about nineteen miles off Abu Dhabi's western coastline, near Qatar. Other islands, such as Das, Al-Mubarraz, Arzanah, and Zirku, have only small populations and are home to facilities for storing and exporting oil and gas. Another island, Sir Bani Yas, is surrounded by water deep enough to accommodate large oil tankers. It is largely unpopulated, however, and since the 1970s has been managed as a wildlife sanctuary and nature reserve.

The second-largest emirate, Dubai, is also located along the gulf coast, just northeast of Abu Dhabi. Like Abu Dhabi, its main geographical feature is desert. However, its coastline features broad, sandy beaches and the only natural harbor on the gulf coast suitable for shipping and trade. The harbor is created by a wide saltwater inlet, called Dubai Creek, that separates the twin port cities of Dubai and

The twin cities of Dubai (pictured) and Dairah have the only natural harbor in the Persian Gulf that is suitable for shipping and trade.

Dairah. Although sandbars frequently build up, Dubai regularly dredges the harbor to keep it open for trade. Dubai also has created other man-made harbors to enhance its maritime trade activities.

Sharjah, the next-largest emirate, borders Dubai to the east and has geography similar to Dubai's. Its Persian Gulf coastline, however, is shorter and has few locations suitable for ports. Sharjah stretches across the narrow Musandam Peninsula, so it also has some shoreline on the Gulf of Oman. This is the location of Khor Fakkan, the main port of the eastern region. Also located in the Gulf of Oman is Abu Musa, an island that is part of Sharjah, which has mineral deposits and some petroleum that has historically provided income for Sharjah.

To the northeast of Sharjah, on the Persian Gulf side of the Musandam Peninsula, are the UAE's two smallest emirates, Ajman and Umm al Qaywayn. Ajman is the smaller of the two; it comprises only about 3 percent of the UAE's territory (only one hundred square miles) and has a population of fewer than one hundred thousand. Its capital and only city, Ajman, is located on the gulf next to a small creek. In addition to a port (also called Ajman), the emirate has an interior agricultural area in the southeast called Masfout which uses water trapped in surrounding mountain valleys for irrigation. Ajman has no known oil reserves but has a number of industrial plants that produce a variety of goods, including foodstuffs, beverages, tobacco, textiles, leather goods, and paper products. Umm al Qaywayn, the second-smallest emirate in terms of land area, is the least populated of all the emirates, with only about forty thousand people. Like Ajman, it lacks oil resources; with a bit of land and small frontage on the gulf, it survives mostly on trade and agriculture.

The UAE's two remaining emirates, Fujairah and Ras al-Khaimah, are located in the northeastern portion of the peninsula. This area is bisected by the Hajar Mountains. These rugged mountains rise as high as sixty-five hundred feet above sea level, and their dominating and craggy peaks present a dramatic change from the comparatively flat desert scenery that makes up much of the UAE. Rainfall in this area runs off and accumulates in deep gorges (called wadis). Because of this accumulation of water, it is also one of the few places in the UAE that stays green most of the

year. This available water supply also supports some agriculture, including a wide variety of fruits and vegetables. The Hajar Mountains drop directly into the sea in the northern part of Fujairah, allowing little direct ocean access. However, the southern part of Fujairah's Oman Gulf coastline contains some of the UAE's most beautiful sand beaches, inspiring the emirate recently to develop some tourist facilities there.

An SUV makes its way through the rugged Hajar Mountains in the northeast. The mountains' peaks offer a striking contrast to the deserts that dominate most of the UAE.

A Desert Climate

The UAE's climate is characterized by heat and sun, with scant rainfall and frequent sandstorms. The hottest months are July and August, when temperatures average 93 degrees Fahrenheit. In the interior deserts, however, temperatures in the summer commonly reach 120 degrees or higher. Only in the Hajar Mountains, because of the altitude, are the summer temperatures slightly cooler. Along the coast, the heat is intensified by a humid southeastern wind known as *sharqi*, which makes for sticky and uncomfortable conditions. As historian Rosemarie Said Zahlan notes, "The combination of heat and humidity produces conditions not dissimilar from those of a steam-bath."[1]

In winter, temperatures are usually more moderate, hovering between 77 and 95 degrees Fahrenheit during the daytime, although they may drop as low as 48 degrees at night.

UAE's BEAUTIFUL BEACHES

The UAE offers tourists some of the most attractive beaches in the world. Long stretches of soft white sand frame the warm blue and turquoise waters of the Persian Gulf. Some of the best beaches can be found in Dubai in an area known as Jumeirah Road. In this area a number of first-class resorts, hotels, and private clubs have been built, but there are also public beaches. Indeed, the UAE has capitalized on its beach treasures by creating public beach parks, which feature amenities such as showers, bathrooms, lush landscaping, restaurants, entertainment, and parking. In Dubai, for example, four beach parks have been built: Jumeirah Beach (featuring a group of green hills next to a white beach and blue ocean), Al-Mumzar (a vast beach park with five beaches, swimming pools, rental bungalows, and barbecues), Al-Safa Park (a serene and heavily landscaped beach park with a games area, a ladies' beach, and a landscaped labyrinth, or maze), and Jumeirah Open Beach Park (a relatively undevel-

oped natural beach with minimal amenities such as showers, toilets, lifeguards, snacks, seating, and landscaping). Despite such attractions, beaches in the UAE are hardly ever crowded.

The UAE offers tourists first-rate resorts and beautiful beaches like this one in Dubai.

Winter is also when the UAE receives its only rainfall, although the amount is usually quite low. Abu Dhabi, with its vast deserts, gets the least amount of rain—an average of only 1.7 inches per year. Areas farther to the northeast, such as Sharjah, get about double that amount of rainfall, while mountainous areas, such as Fujairah and Ras al-Khaimah, receive the most—about 5.1 inches per year. The amount of rainfall, however, varies widely from year to year. In fact, several years may pass in which little or no rain falls. In 1982, however, the UAE experienced record-breaking rains: In one month, more rain fell than in the previous ten years—enough to replenish its depleted underground water sources. Still, rainfall rarely supplies enough water for drinking or industrial uses. To make up the difference, the UAE has built desalination plants that make ocean water drinkable.

The people of the UAE adapt as much as possible to this harsh climate. Virtually all buildings—houses, hotels, government offices, and businesses—are air-conditioned, making it possible for people to live and work in relative comfort. Still, conditions can be difficult. The humid sea air close to the coast wreaks havoc on metal structures and automobiles, corroding them in short order. Away from the coast, violent sandstorms can arise, destroying many objects made of metal or glass, and reducing visibility to the point that travel is hazardous.

PLANTS AND ANIMALS

Better adapted to the harsh conditions are plants and animals that are native to the UAE. A wide variety of grasses and shrubs manage to survive even in the desert. Some have roots deep enough to reach underground sources of water, for example, while others have small leaves to reduce moisture loss; many simply become dormant during dry spells, then come to life when it rains. Along the coast, plants have adapted to the high levels of salt in the soil. One plant species called the tamarix, for example, extracts salt from the water its roots take up, excreting the salt on its thin, needlelike leaves. Other native plants, including palm, acacia, and tamarisk trees, are less drought tolerant and grow naturally only in the oases where underground water makes it possible for them to survive. Other less drought-tolerant shrubs and grasses flourish as a result of the rain in the

Hajar Mountains. However, given the lack of water and the fact that the soil in most areas is almost 100 percent sand, many desert areas of the UAE appear almost barren of life.

Despite the challenges of heat and dryness, the UAE, using underground, recycled, and desalinated water, has in recent years turned many parts of the desert green. Irrigation of land surrounding the major oases and cities, for example, has allowed eucalyptus trees, date palms, decorative plants such as bougainvillea, as well as fruits and vegetables to thrive. Some of these efforts at greening the desert are extensive. For example, Sheikh Zayed bin Sultan al-Nuhayyan has promoted a large tree-planting program. More than 70 million acacias, eucalyptus trees, and palm trees have been planted on more than seven hundred thousand acres in the desert as well as in cities such as al-Ain and the capital city, Abu Dhabi.

Relatively few wildlife species make their homes in the difficult climate in the UAE. Although dozens of varieties of birds can be found, many simply migrate to the area in the winters to feed and nest. Among these are hawks, gulls, and the Indian roller, a bird that is an unremarkable brown color

These acacias are among the more than 70 million trees planted in irrigated areas as part of a government program to introduce trees to the UAE's deserts.

A hunting falcon rests on its perch in Abu Dhabi. Falconry is a very popular pastime in the UAE.

until it flies, when it reveals brilliant, iridescent blue feathers. One bird species that is native is the falcon, which is often caught and trained to hunt prey. In contrast to the barrenness of the land, the gulf waters are rich in marine life, with more than two hundred types of fish, among them edible species such as the snapper and the hamour. Shrimp, sea turtles, and dugongs, or sea cows (a large gray marine mammal), also frequent the coastal waters of the UAE.

The desert supports almost no land animals, however. Among the native species are the oryx and gazelle (two types of small antelope), which were once hunted almost to extinction. In an effort to protect the country's natural treasures, Zayed has made preserving the environment and wildlife a priority, which has helped halt the decline of these and other species.

POPULATION AND CITIES

The UAE's inhospitable climate means that most of the country is sparsely populated, if at all. Largely because so

UAE's Endangered Sea Cow

The UAE is home to the unusual and endangered dugong, or sea cow, a large marine mammal similar to but slightly smaller than the manatee found in Florida waters. The dugong is an ancient creature that shares ancestors with the elephant. Dugongs are smaller than elephants, but full-grown they weigh more than eight hundred pounds and grow to almost ten feet in length. Like elephants, dugongs also have long tusks and live a long time—up to seventy years.

Dugongs have been listed as vulnerable to extinction by the World Conservation Union. Their numbers have shown a marked decline in recent years, most likely the result of human activities. As a species, dugongs may be particularly at risk for extinction because they do not rapidly reproduce; females produce calves only about once every four years. Also, if a mother is killed, her calf will die as well, because it is completely dependent on its mother. Experts on marine animals have yet to learn how to feed a baby dugong, and they have not been able to cultivate the sea grass that forms the diet of dugongs once they are weaned.

much of the countryside is desert that supports little in the way of permanent settlements, about 90 percent of the people live in cities. Moreover, 80 percent of the entire population of the UAE lives in only three coastal cities—Abu Dhabi, Dubai, and Sharjah. The remaining 16 to 20 percent of Emiratis live in larger towns located at oases and in the four smaller emirates. These settlements include al-Ain, Ras al-Khaimah, Fujairah, Ajman, Umm al Qaywayn, Kalba, Khor Fakkan, Dibba, and Dhaid, and the newly created cities of Jebel Ali in the emirate of Dubai and Ruwais in Abu Dhabi. Smaller villages also exist in the mountains and in areas such as Abu Dhabi's Buraimi and Liwa oases.

In addition to being highly urbanized, the country's population is growing rapidly. The population, estimated at eighty thousand to ninety-five thousand in 1960, stood at almost 3 million in 2002. This increase is largely a result of improved health care paid for by oil revenues. This population includes a homogenous Arab citizenry. Although some are descended from the Bedouin, a nomadic people from the desert, and others from the Hadhr, the settled people of the mountain areas and oases, all identify themselves as Arab. They all speak Arabic, the UAE's official language, and virtually all follow Islam, the country's official religion.

In addition to this native Arab populace, as is the case with many oil-rich countries, the UAE is home to large numbers of foreigners. This is because of the need for workers with the skills to run the nation's oil and related industries. Today, despite rapid growth among the native population, foreigners outnumber native Emiratis by more than four to one. Although there are some women among the immigrants, these foreign workers are generally young men between the ages of twenty and forty. Most come from other largely Arab countries and areas, such as Oman, Jordan, Palestine, Egypt, and Yemen, but there are workers from Iran, India, Pakistan, and nations in south Asia as well.

This large number of young men from so many different lands, analyst and diplomat Malcolm C. Peck notes, "give[s] the population a very diverse complexion and a distinctly youthful and male character."[2] The characteristic of youthfulness extends to native Emiratis as well, the result of a high birth rate. These factors combine to give the UAE population an average age of about twenty-seven. Still, the UAE is home to a substantial population of older people. Because of improvements in health care and other benefits of the oil boom, people in the UAE tend to live much longer than their ancestors did. The life expectancy today in the UAE is almost seventy-five years, a figure similar to that of other developed countries.

NATURAL RESOURCES

The oil that brought about demographic changes in the UAE is the major natural resource of the area, providing almost 90 percent of the UAE's income. The other major natural resources in the emirates, and the ones that provided most of the income prior to the discovery of oil, are fish and pearls. Neither of these resources produced great wealth. In contrast, the UAE today is enormously wealthy thanks to oil and its by-product, natural gas.

The supply of these resources is vast. The UAE owns a total of approximately 98 billion barrels of oil—close to 10 percent of the world's proven oil reserves. Abu Dhabi holds the vast majority of these oil reserves—92.2 billion barrels or about 94 percent. Dubai owns an estimated 4 billion barrels, followed by Sharjah, with 1.5 billion, and Ras al-Khaimah, with 100 million. Since the mid-1990s the UAE's proven oil reserves in Abu Dhabi have doubled. New oil fields have been discovered offshore, and the emirate also has been successful at tapping new deposits of oil in existing fields. Overall, the UAE is able to produce 2.5 million barrels of oil per day, which it exports directly to other countries. It has also begun to refine its own oil to produce and export end products such as gasoline, fertilizers, and petrochemicals. Even at the current rate of production, experts predict that the UAE's oil reserves are sufficient to last at least another one hundred years.

In addition, the UAE owns the world's fourth-largest natural gas reserves. The country's gas reserves are estimated at 212 trillion cubic feet. Like oil, most of the natural gas is in Abu Dhabi, with smaller amounts in Sharjah, Dubai, and Ras al-Khaimah. Known natural gas reserves in the UAE are projected to last for about 150–170 years.

An oil rig taps deposits found near the coast of Abu Dhabi. The UAE possesses nearly 10 percent of the world's oil reserves.

DATE PALMS—A MAJOR CROP

The date palm has traditionally been grown in the southern Persian Gulf region, both as a source of food and for export. Dates can be eaten either fresh or packaged; they also are used to make liquid sugar, vinegar, and *dibs* (a type of honey), and are added to some animal feeds. Other parts of the tree are also important. The leaves are often woven into mats, trays, or baskets; the stalks are used for roofing traditional huts; and fibers can be used as twine and rope.

Date palms are the UAE's most important crop, and most of the available land suitable for fruit in the seven emirates is planted with them. Abu Dhabi grows the most palms, but they are also grown by all the other emirates. The UAE has increased production by using modern agricultural technology and intensive planting techniques to fight pests and diseases. The result is that the UAE today grows about 40.7 million date palms. The dates are still important as food and as an export commodity, but the trees also provide the people of the UAE with shade for growing vegetables and with forested areas to ease the heat and barrenness of the desert.

So far, gas resources have remained relatively undeveloped, but the government plans to change this in the future. The UAE uses massive amounts of electricity to allow people to live in air-conditioned comfort, and the government hopes to build more generating plants that use natural gas to provide electricity for its industrial and household consumers. Currently, the UAE exports much of its gas to Japan in liquefied form aboard special ships, but the government also is planning to build pipelines to link the UAE with neighboring countries Oman and Qatar, which will allow gas to be piped directly to those countries.

OTHER INDUSTRY

The UAE's leadership is aware that petroleum is a finite resource and in recent years has tried to diversify and develop its economy to reduce its dependence on fossil fuel sales. The government has invested in industries such as aluminum production, tourism, aviation, and telecommunications. For example, as part of its push to develop tourism, the UAE has built new hotels, restaurants, and shopping centers, and has expanded its airports. Also, as part of its economic development efforts, the government has sought to sell industries it owns to private investors, who it hopes will bring fresh ideas and funding to increase production and efficiency. In 1998, for example, the government undertook an initiative to privatize the country's water and electricity businesses. In addition, the government has enacted laws that make the UAE a friendly business climate that encourages foreign investments.

These efforts have been relatively successful. The nonoil portions of the UAE's economy have grown to about 30 percent of its total exports and about 70 percent of its gross domestic product (GDP), the total market value of all goods and services produced in a country in a given year. However, there have been problems coordinating economic activities among the seven emirates, because they often seem to compete with each other. This is a legacy of the nation's past, before the emirates charted a new political course by creating a new nation.

The Journey
to Prosperity

As recently as the 1950s, the area now called the UAE was completely undeveloped, one of the poorest regions of the world. Its inhabitants lived as their ancestors did, moving with their herds across the desert or eking out a meager existence as fishermen, traders, or pearl divers. Each of the seven emirates was ruled by a powerful tribal sheikh and although some merchants grew wealthy from trading in pearls, most people lived in poverty. However, a fortune in the form of oil lay just under the sand and sea. This resource, once discovered, would rapidly transform their lands into a place of enormous wealth and promise.

Life Before Oil

Before the discovery of oil, most people in what today is the UAE struggled just to survive. All the emirates lacked sufficient water and good soil necessary for farming. The Persian Gulf teemed with fish, and thus many people made their living as fishermen. In addition, the sea bottom was home to oysters, which produced pearls. Merchants provided the funding to buy and equip a boat, and divers would swim as deep as 130 feet to collect the oysters and bring them to the surface, where they were opened to expose the pearls. The pearling industry, in fact, became the area's most important and lucrative industry. As authors Eric Hooglund and Anthony Toth explain, "Pearls from the rich banks off the Emirates' coast were probably the single largest source of wealth until the 1930s and 1940s. In 1905 the pearling trade involved 22,000 men from the [Emirates] working in about 1,300 boats."[3] The pearling season lasted from May to September and was very dangerous; many divers would

Before the discovery of oil in the mid-1950s, the harvesting of pearls was the most important industry in the UAE.

drown or suffer lung damage before they could return to the surface. Others suffered agonizing deaths from shark attacks. Despite the risks they took, most involved in pearling made very little money, although the merchants who financed the operations became very wealthy and powerful. The merchants, in turn, provided part of this income to the rulers of the tribes, known as sheikhs.

Other coastal people became seafarers, traders, and boatbuilders in ancient seaports such as Sharjah and Dubai. A few people mined small deposits of red oxide, a substance used to make paint and cosmetics, on some of the gulf islands. In addition, some people took advantage of relatively abundant water in the Liwa and Buraimi oases and the plateaus of the mountainous emirate of Ras al-Khaimah. At these locations, farmers grew crops such as date palms and grains. The wells of the oases also provided water for the nomadic Bedouin population, who traveled with their animal herds throughout the desert in search of seasonal grazing areas.

Although the lives of the nomadic, mountain, and coastal people differed dramatically, they shared a belief in Islam, a religion that had swept through the Arab world in the middle of the seventh century A.D. Islam united this part of the world not just in terms of faith, but economically as well. As Peck explains, "Islam had the effect . . . of bringing both coasts of the Gulf under Arab Muslim rule. This led to the period of the greatest flowering of Gulf commerce with India and China, under both Arab and Persian merchants, from the seventh to the tenth centuries A.D."[4]

THE BRITISH INFLUENCE

In later centuries, the trade the Arabs of the gulf region engaged in brought them into direct competition—and conflict —with larger European powers. The Europeans wanted to monopolize trade routes through the gulf, and take over the rich trade with India and the Far East. As early as the sixteenth century, Portugal seized territories in the region, including the port of Khor Fakkan, which today is in the emirate of Sharjah, and the island of Hormuz on the northern side of the Persian Gulf. Holding these two small territories allowed Portugal to control the Strait of Hormuz, the entrance to the Persian Gulf. No ship could pass through

ARAB PIRACY

Stories of Arab piracy in the Persian Gulf in the early nineteenth century are the subject of debate among historians. Clearly, there was an increase in the number of attacks on ships traveling in the gulf at this time, a large number of which were attributed to the Qawasim, a coastal tribal federation based in the areas now occupied by Sharjah and Ras al-Khaimah. The Qawasim forces included more than sixty large ships, several hundred smaller boats, and about twenty thousand skilled sailors and fighters. Their ships were fast and maneuverable. Some of their attacks were directed against other Arabs, but some English ships were also targets. The British at the time and most Westerners since then have referred to these attackers as pirates. Arabs, on the other hand, tend to describe the attacks as "maritime warfare," and contend that the British actions to control the gulf region are more aptly described as piracy than are the activities of the Qawasim. Most scholars agree, however, that much of the maritime violence at this time in the gulf was caused by efforts by the Qawasim to seize a larger share of the gulf trade—trade that had been dominated by Oman for many years and that was increasingly including British and Western ships. Unfortunately for the Qawasim, the British joined forces with Oman and were able to decisively destroy the Qawasim seafaring operation.

the strait without the knowledge and permission of Portugal. In 1622, however, Britain, backed by Persian allies, captured the island, breaking Portugal's stranglehold on the trade route. By the late 1700s Britain had emerged as the most powerful presence in the region. The British East India Company, which had been given a monopoly on trade with India by the British king, dominated the gulf trading routes and acted as an agent for the British government in its relations with other countries and peoples. Given the importance of its trade with India, Britain came to think of the Persian Gulf as essential to its economic security.

During the early 1800s, however, that security was threatened by a group of Arab tribes known as the Qawasim. The Qawasim owned a large fleet of ships, equipped for both trading and warfare, and commanded thousands of fighting

This illustration depicts a ship in the British East India Company's fleet. By the late 1700s the company controlled all of the Persian Gulf trading routes.

men. Based in Sharjah and Ras al-Khaimah, they routinely attacked and pillaged British ships. The Qawasim's motives were both economic and political. In addition to being a rival to control trade in the region, Britain was friendly with tribal enemies of the Qawasim based in Oman. To the British, the Qawasim were simply pirates. British military forces attacked the Qawasim's main headquarters in Ras al-Khaimah and destroyed their fleet of ships, soundly defeating them in 1819.

Following this victory, Britain negotiated a peace treaty with the Qawasim and the rulers of various tribal sheikhdoms in the gulf region, including Abu Dhabi, Dubai, Ajman, Umm al Qaywayn, and Bahrain. In the 1820 treaty, known as the General Treaty of Peace, each ruling sheikh promised not to engage in piracy and to allow safe passage for British ships. In return, Britain agreed not to interfere in the sheikhs' local affairs. Later, in 1835, Britain encouraged the sheikhs to sign a second treaty in which the tribes agreed to end warfare with neighboring tribes and to give Britain the authority to maintain the peace in the region. This treaty subsequently evolved into a permanent treaty called the Perpetual Maritime Truce of 1853. Thereafter, as historian Zahlan describes, "The states whose rulers had signed the Perpetual Maritime Truce became known [in Europe] as Trucial states."[5] This Trucial system secured peaceful shipping conditions in the Persian Gulf and placed the Trucial States firmly under British influence.

At the same time, the 1820 and 1835 treaties benefited the tribal rulers. For the first time, the tribal sheikhs were recognized as independent rulers who could enter into agreements with foreign powers. This recognition strengthened tribal leaders, greatly affecting the area's history. As Peck explains, "It did so by freezing the power relationships that existed between tribes or tribal confederations, thereby preserving a number of small states that otherwise would probably have been swallowed by larger neighbors."[6]

Later, Britain tightened its control over the Trucial States, after other powers such as the Ottoman Empire, France, Russia, and Germany sought to establish relationships with the ruling sheikhs. This tightening of control culminated in the Treaty of 1892, in which the sheikhs of the Trucial States agreed not to negotiate or make agreements with any foreign power without Britain's consent; in return, Britain promised military protection. This arrangement greatly increased British power in the area and at the same time isolated the Trucial States from the rest of the world. It also, like the earlier treaties, strengthened tribal sheikhs and preserved their separate sheikhdoms. As Zahlan explains, "[British policy] contributed to the strengthening of the respective positions of the different rulers. Government was left entirely to them so long as they fulfilled their treaty obligation. . . . The fact that Britain had separate relations with all the states, large or small, encouraged feelings of separation between them."[7]

THE TRUCIAL SHEIKHDOMS

British involvement in the Trucial States or sheikhdoms also had the effect of transferring power from coastal tribal leaders to inland tribes. The Qawasim, after all, were coastal tribes, and with their defeat, a rival group of inland tribes called the Bani Yas rose in power.

The Bani Yas tribesmen traditionally were either nomadic herdsmen or farmed in the oases of the region. Bani Yas tribal sheikhs ruled Abu Dhabi from their headquarters in the Liwa Oasis. In 1761 the discovery of freshwater on Abu Dhabi Island had made possible a permanent settlement there. Some of the Bani Yas took advantage of this opportunity and became coastal fishermen and pearl traders. The Bani Yas also expanded their rule to the Buraimi Oasis. By the end of the nineteenth century, the success of the Bani Yas had made Abu Dhabi the dominant power in the Trucial States.

Meanwhile, however, the Qawasim sheikhs continued to maintain a stronghold in the northern area of the Trucial States. There, in the rugged mountains, they were able to fend off attempts by the Bani Yas to dominate them militarily. Various Qawasim tribal members settled and gained control over areas such as Sharjah, Ras al-Khaimah, and at the villages of Dibba and Kalba on the coast of the Oman Gulf.

Later, some of the Bani Yas, under leaders such as Maktum bin Buti, broke away from the tribe and established settlements in neighboring Dubai. This venture was successful; despite threats from both the Bani Yas and the Qawasim, the new Dubai sheikhdom survived and, with its excellent natural harbor, became a leading center of trade on the gulf. By the early twentieth century, after years of rivalries and instability, five relatively peaceful Trucial sheikhdoms, or emirates—Abu Dhabi, Dubai, Sharjah (which at this time was united with Ras al-Khaimah), Umm al Qaywayn, and Ajman—had been established.

OIL DISCOVERIES

The relative peace among the Trucial States did not, however, result in prosperity for the majority of the people in the gulf. In fact, poverty worsened due to events in the 1930s that decimated the Trucial States' pearl industry. First, a worldwide economic depression that began in 1929 reduced the demand for luxury items such as pearls. Of greater long-term significance, the Japanese developed techniques for cultivating oysters—and therefore pearls—in shallow water, eliminating the need for arduous dives into oyster beds in deep water. These shallow-water pearls could be sold much more cheaply than those collected from the gulf waters. Their livelihoods destroyed by the drop in

DUBAI'S REFORM MOVEMENT

During the period between World War I and World War II, a period when Britain exercised great control over the relatively undeveloped gulf region, the Trucial State of Dubai experienced a political movement that sought to reform the government and improve the social and economic conditions there. The movement for reform was led by members of the extended family of Dubai's ruler, Sheikh Maktum bin Hashar, who helped Dubai prosper (in the days before oil) as a center for the pearling and reexport trade. When economic conditions declined in the 1930s and the pearl industry was faced with destruction by competition from Japanese cultured pearls, much of Dubai's wealth also disappeared. The depressed economic conditions led to the reform movement, which in 1938 forced Maktum to accept the creation of a consultative council designed to provide advice to the ruler about political and social improvements. Over the next few months, this system was successful in expanding Dubai's harbor and establishing the first real schools in the Trucial States. Although Maktum was able to dissolve the council after only five months, its success provided an example that Dubai later followed to generate even greater reforms and economic development.

the price of pearls, many men migrated to the nearby countries of Kuwait, Bahrain, and later Qatar and Saudi Arabia, where they found work in newly developed oil fields.

By the mid-1930s the Trucial States were seeking to tap into suspected oil reserves of their own. In 1937 Dubai's ruler, Sheikh Saeed, granted a company known as the Petroleum Concessions Ltd. the right to explore for oil. That same year, Sharjah granted a similar concession to the company. The leaders of Ras al-Khaimah, Abu Dhabi, and Ajman followed suit. These agreements had two immediate consequences. First, because the agreements were made in the names of the various tribal sheiks, the sheikhs' power was greatly enhanced. Second, the agreements raised questions about the boundaries of each sheikhdom, since oil companies needed to know whose territory they were in when they drilled for oil. As a consequence, a series of territorial disputes, both among the Trucial emirates (particularly Abu Dhabi and Dubai) and between them and neighboring countries such as Saudi Arabia, broke out. The outbreak of World War II in 1939, however, interrupted plans for oil exploration and delayed resolution of these disputes.

After the war ended in 1945, Britain helped to resolve disputes among the Trucial States and facilitate efforts to drill for oil. For example, in 1951 a security force, eventually called the Trucial Oman Scouts, was formed by the British in Sharjah. The Scouts' purpose was to maintain peace in the Trucial States and provide security for oil workers. In 1952, to help unify the ruling sheikhs, the British created the Trucial States Council (TSC), a body with representatives from each of the seven Trucial emirates (now including Fujairah and Ras al-Khaimah). Although the TSC had only advisory powers, it provided a venue in which rulers could meet to discuss matters that affected them all.

Not long after the establishment of the TSC, an event occurred that greatly changed the economic picture for at least some of the Trucial emirates. In 1959, after several unsuccessful attempts, the first big oil strike was made off the coast of Abu Dhabi. By 1963 these wells were producing significant revenues for the emirate. Offshore oil strikes were followed by even richer finds on land. Meanwhile, oil was also discovered in neighboring emirates. In 1960 a large oil reserve was discovered in Dubai, giving it significant oil

wealth by 1970. Oil would later be discovered in two other areas, producing oil revenues for Sharjah by 1975 and for Ras al-Khaimah by 1984. Other emirates—Ajman, Umm al Qaywayn, and Fujairah—also granted drilling concessions, but no oil was found.

OIL WEALTH AND ECONOMIC DEVELOPMENT

Oil fueled economic development in the emirates where it was found. Under the leadership of Sheikh Rashid bin Said al-Maktum, for example, Dubai was able to fund public services, such as electricity and police protection. Dubai also worked to upgrade its ports and other trade facilities, quickly becoming the economic and trade leader in the region. Abu Dhabi, despite its greater wealth, initially proceeded much more slowly, fearing that quick modernization might destroy its traditional desert culture. Rapid development began, however, when Sheikh Zayed bin Sultan al-Nuhayyan came to power in 1966. Under Zayed's leadership, the emirate created a system of health and social services and made plans for public works. Zayed also expanded Abu

British soldiers in the Trucial States during World War II take cover as a bomb explodes. After the war, the British helped the Trucial States establish a profitable oil industry.

THE BURAIMI DISPUTE

Oil exploration in an oasis area of Abu Dhabi known as Buraimi in 1949 created a serious dispute with Saudi Arabia over the boundary line between the two territories. At that time, King Abdul Aziz bin al-Saud of Saudi Arabia contended that the whole inland area of the eastern Arabian Peninsula belonged to his kingdom. Britain, however, defended Abu Dhabi's claims to these desert areas, and a joint British-Saudi commission was established in Buraimi 1951 to try to settle the dispute. When discussions failed, both sides sent troops to take control of Buraimi. A military confrontation was avoided when the British and Saudis agreed to create an international tribunal to decide the issue. This tribunal, however, also failed to find a solution, prompting Abu Dhabi and Oman, with Britain's encouragement, to occupy Buraimi militarily and repel Saudi forces in 1955. Britain then unilaterally imposed a border thereafter referred to as the Riyadh Line. The border dispute festered quietly until after the UAE achieved independence, when it resurfaced as one of the UAE's first foreign policy challenges. The dispute was finally resolved in 1974, when the UAE's president, Sheikh Zayed, ne-

gotiated an accord with then Saudi king Faisal bin Abdul Aziz al-Saud that, among other things, provided for the two countries to share certain oil revenues from the region.

King Faisal bin Abdul Aziz al-Saud of Saudi Arabia was instrumental in resolving the Buraimi dispute.

Dhabi's defense forces, which soon outnumbered Sharjah's Trucial Oman Scouts.

Other emirates, lacking resources to pay for similar modernization efforts, trailed far behind Dubai and Abu Dhabi in their standard of living. Hope for these poorer emirates at first seemed to come from the Arab League, a group of oil-rich Arab countries that created a fund to pay for development projects in these areas. However, Britain, threatened by what it considered as interference from these other nations, refused to permit Arab League delegations to enter the Trucial States and enforced this decision with strong action, including deposing the ruler of Sharjah after he invited the Arab League to the area. Instead, Britain set up its own development fund (as part of the TSC), to which it contributed an initial grant. The emirates with oil revenues were then expected to make contributions to the fund. Abu Dhabi, with its large oil wealth, contributed the largest share to the fund, making development possible in areas other than Dubai and Abu Dhabi. For example, a system of modern schools was created in Sharjah and Ras al-Khaimah; other development initiatives included road construction, health services, housing, utilities, and telephone service.

The TSC and the development fund encouraged the Trucial States to work together to solve their problems. As political scientist Ali Mohammed Khalifa describes, "Rulers could and did, for the first time in the history of their relations, exchange ideas as a group on a face-to-face basis. This helped over the years in the emergence of some sort of consensus in the tackling of problems of common concern."[8]

BRITISH WITHDRAWAL

The new oil wealth and the experiences with the TSC and the development fund fostered more positive relationships among the Trucial States and prepared them for greater political autonomy. Yet there was no compelling reason for them to change what by then had become a comfortable relationship with Britain. Instead, it was Britain itself that made the decision to end its domination of politics in the gulf.

Britain's decision to withdraw from the gulf was largely financial. By the late 1960s, as a result of economic problems at home, maintaining its Middle East military presence became increasingly unaffordable for Britain. As scholar

Malcolm Yapp put it, "a blow in the pocket thrust Britain from the Gulf."[9] Other factors contributing to the British decision to leave the region included Britain's loss of its Far East trade empire (after India gained its independence), its access to secure sources of oil elsewhere in the Middle East, and the fact that an ally, the United States, was quickly increasing its influence in the region. On January 16, 1968, Britain abruptly announced it was withdrawing from the Persian Gulf by the end of 1971.

The British announcement caught the world by surprise and caused great concern among the Trucial States, who felt suddenly abandoned. As former UAE minister Abdullah Omran Taryam notes, "Some of the rulers genuinely wanted Britain not to withdraw. . . . Some even offered to bear the cost of the British military presence in the area . . . an offer to this effect was made by Sheikh Zayed, the Ruler of Abu Dhabi, who could pay from his oil revenues, and a similar offer came from Sheikh Rashid, the Ruler of Dubai."[10]

Rulers in the gulf and observers around the world worried that Britain's withdrawal would leave the Trucial States unprotected and open to aggression by larger nations hungry for their oil riches. Iran, in particular, seemed inclined to take advantage of the power vacuum to dominate the Trucial sheikhdoms. In addition, the ruling sheikhs seemed unprepared to work together in a meaningful way. Although they had some recent experiences with unified decision making in the TSC, they had openly warred and competed with each other for hundreds of years, and few people expected that would change overnight. As journalist David Holden declared at the time, "there is no realistic possibility of the present Gulf rulers coming together of their own accord in any political grouping worth mentioning."[11]

INDEPENDENCE

Despite these dire predictions, the Trucial States, led by Sheikh Zayed of Abu Dhabi and Sheikh Rashid of Dubai, began discussions aimed at welding the various Gulf sheikhdoms together into a single nation. The first tangible product of these negotiations was an agreement signed by Zayed and Rashid on February 18, 1968, to create a federation between Abu Dhabi and Dubai. Neighboring sheikhdoms were then invited to join. The two sheikhs first proposed a federation of nine, which would have included the seven emirates that now comprise the UAE plus two nearby states —Qatar and Bahrain. All nine rulers met and quickly agreed to form a federation in the Dubai Agreement of 1968. However, Bahrain and Qatar eventually opted instead to become independent nations, and the emirate of Ras al-Khaimah wavered on joining the proposed federation, objecting to certain representation and budget provisions of the pact.

The remaining six emirates went ahead with the plan for a federation, which was officially declared on July 18, 1971. The declaration statement said: "In response to the desire of our Arab people, we, the rulers of Abu Dhabi, Dubai, Sharjah, Ajman, Umm Al-Qaiwain and Fujairah, have resolved

Sheikh Zayed, leader of Abu Dhabi, signs the document creating the United Arab Emirates in 1971.

to establish a federal state under the name of the United Arab Emirates."[12] On December 2, 1971, one day after Britain formally ended its treaties with them, the six emirates issued their formal declaration of independence. Each emirate agreed to contribute 10 percent of its income to finance the federation. Zayed was elected president, Rashid was elected vice president, and Sheikh Maktum bin Rashid, the crown prince of Dubai, was appointed prime minister. Shortly thereafter, in February 1972, the government of Ras al-Khaimah decided to join the federation. Thus, the seven-member union was complete, and the modern United Arab Emirates was born.

3

Unity and Progress

After achieving its independence, the UAE faced many challenges, both internal and external. Some of these were immediate threats from neighboring countries. Others related to questions of how to actually unify seven different political entities and how to divide the new oil wealth fairly. Largely through leadership and consensus building, the UAE defied initial predictions that it would not survive and succeeded in surmounting many of these problems.

The Federation Government

The federation created by the UAE's declaration of independence is a system in which a central government is given certain specified powers, leaving all other powers to the individual emirates. The provisional, or temporary, constitution adopted by the seven emirates on December 2, 1971, called for the federal government to be responsible mostly for foreign affairs and defense. The federal government was also given responsibility for some domestic matters, such as education, public health and medical services, money and currency, collection of taxes, air traffic control, citizenship and immigration, road building, and communication services.

The emirates, however, were careful to limit the federal government's power. The ruling sheikhs did not fully trust each other and each wanted to retain for himself as much power as possible. Section 3 of the constitution, therefore, specifically stated that "the member emirates shall exercise sovereignty over their respective territories . . . in all matters not pertaining to the union."[13] Similarly, other sections of the constitution specified that individual emirates retained

35

SHEIKH ZAYED BIN SULTAN AL-NUHAYYAN

In 2001 Sheikh Zayed bin Sultan al-Nuhayyan celebrated thirty-five years as ruler of the emirate of Abu Dhabi, and was reelected as president of the UAE, a post he has held since December 1971. Born in about 1918 (the date is uncertain), Zayed is the grandson of the famous Sheikh Zayed bin Khalifa al-Nuhayyan (Zayed the Great), a Bani Yas tribesman who ruled Abu Dhabi from 1855 to 1909, the longest reign in the emirate's history. Zayed's father, Sheikh Sultan, ruled Abu Dhabi between 1922 and 1926, followed by his uncle and then his eldest brother, Sheikh Shakhbut.

Growing up, Zayed knew Abu Dhabi as a poor and undeveloped place. He was given reading and writing instruction by a religious tutor and spent much of his youth in the desert, where he lived among the Bedouin, absorbing their traditions, values, and respect for nature. His rapport with the people led his brother to appoint him to govern the town of al-Ain, at the Buraimi Oasis, and later when oil was discovered, he was put in charge of Abu Dhabi's oil exploration. In these positions, Zayed quickly developed a reputation for leadership and patient mediation of disputes. On August 6, 1966, he was the natural choice to succeed his brother as ruler of Abu Dhabi. As the key leader in the formation of the UAE, he was selected as its president in 1971, and today he is respected around the world for his leadership and vision in developing the UAE into a successful and stable nation. Now about ninety and in deteriorating health, Zayed has named his son, Sheikh Khalifah, to succeed him.

the right to make agreements with neighboring states and countries, to decide whether to join international bodies such as the Organization of Petroleum Exporting Countries (OPEC), to maintain their own political systems, and to manage their natural resources. The emirates even reserved the right to establish individual armed forces.

The constitution also created three federal governing bodies—the Supreme Federal Council (called the SFC or simply the Supreme Council), the Council of Ministers, and the Federal National Council (FNC). The SFC is the highest executive authority, consisting of the rulers of the seven emirates, and elects the UAE's president and vice president from among its members. It also must approve the federal budget and all national laws and international treaties. The ruler of each of the seven emirates has one vote, and all important decisions require five votes, two of which must be those of Dubai and Abu Dhabi, the two largest emirates. In addition, the president and vice president are given the power to veto any of the SFC's decisions.

The laws on which the SFC passes judgment are made by the Council of Ministers, whose members are appointed by the ruling emirs. With its combination of executive and legislation functions, the council is responsible for the day-to-day business of governing the UAE. It consists of the prime minister, the deputy prime minister, and various other ministers who are in charge of functions such as foreign affairs, defense, public health, and so on. In addition to making most laws, the Council of Ministers formulates the regulations needed to implement those laws. The Council of Ministers

Sheikh Zayed bin Sultan al-Nuhayyan has been the UAE's president since the country was founded in 1971.

also prepares the federal budget and carries out all the decisions of the federal government.

The third body, the FNC, is an advisory council and has few real powers. It does not make laws, only recommendations on laws proposed by the Council of Ministers. It is made up of forty members chosen by the seven emirates. Abu Dhabi and Dubai each have eight seats, Sharjah and Ras al-Khaimah each have six seats, and the other emirates have four seats each. There is also a judiciary made up of a Supreme Court and several lower courts. The Supreme Court, whose judges are appointed by the president and ap-

THE *MAJLIS* TRADITION

Although the UAE is not a democracy and its citizens do not vote for representatives in government, the country continues to rely on a traditional form of political participation called the *majlis*, which means council in Arabic. Traditionally, tribal rulers in the emirates maintained contact with their people, and retained their loyalty and support, by frequently holding an open *majlis* in which tribesmen could voice their opinions. This type of system has been called direct democracy because it allows people a direct voice in government.

Despite the significantly larger population, which makes the *majlis* more difficult to organize, it is still used in the UAE today. Before his health deteriorated, for example, Sheikh Zayed frequently traveled throughout the country to meet with citizens. Rulers of other emirates, or senior members of royal families, also continue to hold open *majlises* in their territories. At these meetings, citizens may comment or make requests on a wide variety of issues—everything from asking for a scholarship for a son or daughter to study abroad to complaints about government ministries. Indeed, because routine government matters are now largely handled by government institutions, traditional *majlises* often focus on very complex issues. It is common, for example, for citizens and sheikhs to have detailed, and sometimes heated, discussions about policy questions, such as the impact of immigration on society or how the UAE should handle relations with neighboring countries. In this way, the *majlises* provide a place where issues can be debated to form a consensus that may lead to legislation or policy changes.

proved by the Supreme Council, hears and decides disputes between individual emirates and the federal government. The lower courts have jurisdiction in disputes between individuals and the federal government, and over other matters such as cases in which someone is accused of a federal crime. All other judicial matters are left to local courts set up by the individual emirates.

This system of government means that there is no popular vote in the UAE; political parties do not exist. Because the ruling sheikhs from the seven emirates form the Supreme Council and choose the president, the ministers, and FNC members, they have virtually complete control over government. In essence, the political leadership in the UAE is tribal, since it is in the hands of men whose families have ruled their respective tribes for generations. As scholar Hassan Hamdan al-Alkim notes, "[ruling families] have retained for themselves the right to control the decision-making process."[14]

Under this system, then, the vast majority of citizens have little or no means of influencing their government. The one exception is a traditional institution called the *majlis*, in which male citizens may meet directly with the ruling sheikh to complain about problems or ask for the government's help. According to Peck, this system seems to work well for the people of the UAE: "[Although] it is far removed from Western political democracy, it nevertheless represents a highly effective form of social democracy that has retained its essential vitality and viability to the present time."[15]

THE IRANIAN THREAT

The first test of the new government resulted from an external threat. Immediately following the UAE's declaration of unity in July 1971, Iran took advantage of the unstable situation to seize three islands—Abu Musa (part of Sharjah), Lesser Tunb, and Greater Tunb (both part of Ras al-Khaimah). The islands' location near the Strait of Hormuz give them strategic importance; whoever occupies them can control access to the Persian Gulf. Although the islands had always been part of Qawasim tribal territories, Iran had periodically tried to occupy the islands as part of its bid to extend its power over the southern gulf area.

In the past, Britain had defended the islands as part of Sharjah and Ras al-Khaimah. This time, however, Britain did

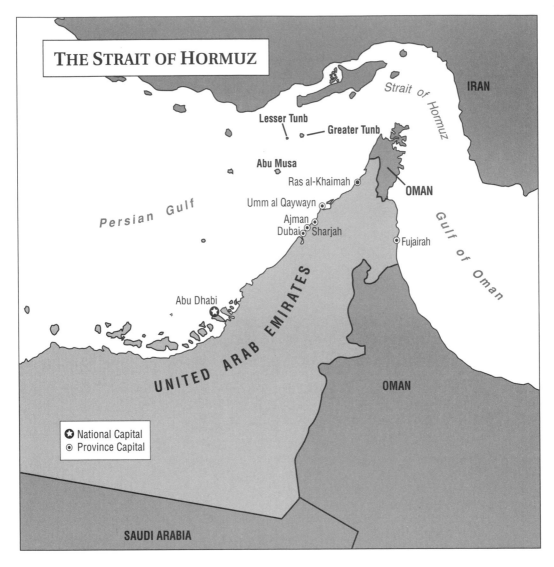

not oppose Iran but instead urged Sharjah and Ras al-Khaimah to negotiate a solution. Britain felt comfortable allowing Iran, which at that time was closely allied with the United States and the West, to control access to the gulf. With no help from Britain in the offing, Sharjah was left with little choice but to sign an agreement with Iran, called the Abu Musa Accord. Under the accord, Sharjah's sovereignty over the island would continue, but Iran would be allowed to deploy troops to the island and share its oil revenues. Similarly, Britain did not defend Ras al-Khaimah's claim to the islands of Lesser and Greater Tunb, allowing Iranian forces to occupy them. The islands were therefore lost to Iran, and they would remain a source of tension between the UAE and Iran for decades to come.

Another serious external threat came from Saudi Arabia, which, soon after the UAE's independence, renewed its historical claim over large portions of Abu Dhabi that held most of the emirate's land-based oil reserves. The Abu Dhabi–Saudi border had been set by Britain in 1955, but Saudi Arabia had never accepted it. Saudi king Faisal bin Abdul Aziz al-Saud refused to recognize the UAE federation government until the dispute with Abu Dhabi was settled, denying the new country much-needed regional support. Finally, in 1974, the dispute was resolved; by giving up some territory, Zayed was able to negotiate an accord that allowed Abu Dhabi to keep the Buraimi Oasis. The pact also provided for Abu Dhabi and Saudi Arabia to share income from the Zarara oil field, located along the emirate's border with Saudi Arabia.

Zayed helped to resolve similar border quarrels between Oman and various emirates (particularly Abu Dhabi) over the Buraimi area and the town of al-Ain, and between Oman and Ras al-Khaimah over the mountain region. Yet another border incident occurred in 1977, when the ruling sheikh of Ras al-Khaimah tried to take over Oman's offshore oil fields. The sheik's forces, however, included many Omanis; they refused to attack, forcing the sheikh to back down.

DIFFICULTIES WITH UNITY

Just as challenging was the need to maintain unity among the seven previously separate emirates. The federation-style constitution did not change the essentially tribal nature of relations in the region, so rivalries and disputes between the ruling sheikhs over borders and resources continued as they always had. Moreover, the sheikhs jealously guarded the sovereignty of their own emirates. One of the first tests came only a month after independence, when Sharjah's ruler, Sheikh Khalid bin Muhammad, was assassinated in a coup attempt mounted by a cousin. The new federal government intervened and successfully installed a new ruler. This action helped show that the federation could overcome threats to its unity.

Federal unity was challenged later in 1972 in a dispute between Sharjah and neighboring Fujairah. The ruler of Fujairah, Sheikh Muhammad al-Shargui, announced that he was presenting UAE president Zayed with an orchard in his territory as a gift. The orchard, however, was watered by a well that had been used for years by residents of both Sharjah and Fujairah, leading to armed conflict between the two emirates. The fighting left twenty people dead and was halted only when troops from Abu Dhabi were stationed in the area to ensure continued sharing of the well.

More difficult to resolve was a dispute between Dubai and Sharjah that began in 1975 when Sharjah wanted to build a shopping center on land claimed by Dubai. This dispute continued for many years and was settled only when the two sides submitted to arbitration by an outside party.

Sheikh Khalid bin Muhammad of Sharjah (front, center) was assassinated in a 1972 coup, just one month after the UAE achieved independence.

Sheikh Rashid of Dubai sought to preserve a large degree of autonomy for his emirate in order to protect its profitable maritime trade from government interference.

A major dispute also emerged between Abu Dhabi and Dubai. Despite the fact that these two emirates were the main advocates of the federation that created the UAE in the first place, they had been rivals in the past and their leaders had very different ideas about how much power should be awarded the new federal government. Zayed, whose Abu Dhabi oil wealth largely subsidized the federation, continually pushed for a strong federal government. Sheikh Rashid of Dubai, on the other hand, sought to retain more local power, in order to pursue Dubai's traditional maritime trade and other economic ventures without federal interference. Dubai, which had significantly smaller oil reserves than Abu Dhabi, was also reluctant to contribute its share of federal expenses, viewing the federal government as a needless bureaucracy.

These differences between the two emirates led in 1976 to a major political crisis for the UAE. Rashid and other ruling sheikhs refused to ratify a draft of a constitution that would have strengthened the federal government and required Dubai to increase its federal contribution. In response, Zayed threatened not to accept another term as UAE's president. To convince him to remain as president, Rashid and the other rulers agreed to certain concessions aimed at meeting his demands for a stronger federal government. One of these concessions provided, for the first time, for the emirates' security and defense forces to be unified into one federal armed force.

THE UAE'S 1996 CONSTITUTION

In 1996 the UAE amended its 1971 constitution to make it permanent. In addition to providing for the nation's five federal institutions (the president, the Supreme Council, the Council of Ministers, the National Council, and the judiciary) and setting forth powers given to the federal government and reserved for the emirates, the constitution contains certain provisions that give the UAE the option of strengthening the federal government as the country grows and evolves. For example, one provision permits the rulers of the emirates to voluntarily give up certain areas of their authority to the federal government if they so choose; this was the basis for a decision in the mid-1970s to unify the emirates' armed forces into one federal military force (although the emirates still maintain some control over the forces they contribute). The constitution also permits each emirate to decide whether to become a member of the Organization of Petroleum Exporting Countries (OPEC); in 1971 Abu Dhabi relied on this option to give up its membership in OPEC in favor of a federal OPEC membership. Another area in which the emirates have slowly given much of their authority to the federal government is the judiciary. Finally, federal power was increased by an amendment passed in 2004 that gives the federal government the power to delegate legislative authority to federal organizations, such as the newly formed Dubai International Financial Center (DIFC).

Other provisions of the constitution prohibit unlawful arrest, search, detention, imprisonment, and home searches, and provide for freedom of speech and equality before the law with regard to race, nationality, religious beliefs, or social status. Amendments to the constitution can be drafted by the Supreme Council and must be approved by a two-thirds majority of the National Council.

However, this agreement was weak and many other federal issues, such as integration of economic and immigration policies, were not resolved. In fact, the issue of how strong the federal government should become would continue to be debated within the UAE for years to come.

These and similar disputes among the emirates prevented agreement on a permanent constitution. Instead, the provisional constitution, adopted in 1971, was extended for five-year periods in 1976, 1981, 1986, and 1991. Finally, however, in June 1996 the UAE approved a permanent constitution. It established Abu Dhabi as the UAE's permanent national capital and essentially made permanent the terms of the provisional constitution.

ECONOMIC PROBLEMS AND SUCCESSES

Disagreements among the emirates were further fueled by uneven economic development resulting from their large differences in income. Since they owned the bulk of the country's oil reserves, Abu Dhabi and Dubai were the wealthiest of the emirates by far. As a result, the burden of paying for the UAE's economic development fell primarily on them. These two states contributed to a federal fund, which was used to build a first-class road system linking the seven emirates, to create a modern telecommunications system, and to develop a social welfare program to provide generous health care, education, food, and housing benefits to all UAE citizens. Much of the federal money was directed toward developing the five oil-poor emirates; in 1976, for example, federal ministries were directed to spend 82 percent of the infrastructure budget on the five emirates with little or no oil.

Yet, despite efforts to redistribute the oil revenues, Abu Dhabi and Dubai, simply because of their great wealth, were able to develop to a much larger extent than the five poorer emirates. This disparity increased in later decades as new oil discoveries gave Abu Dhabi even greater oil and gas reserves. Indeed, even after making a huge federal contribution, Abu Dhabi became enormously wealthy, allowing it to actively develop its industries; build luxurious resorts, airports, and seaports; and spend money on monumental works of architecture, agriculture, and on protecting the environment. Similarly, Dubai had the resources from both trade and oil to pursue an ambitious development plan that included major dock and port facilities, desalination plants, airports, and industrial projects.

By comparison, the smaller, northern emirates lagged far behind in economic development. Since they relied on funds donated by Abu Dhabi and Dubai, economic downturns in the 1980s and 1990s (triggered by events such as drops in oil prices, an eight-year war between Iran and Iraq, and the Iraqi invasion of Kuwait) further heightened economic differences between the oil and nonoil emirates. The slowdowns reduced oil revenues, produced budget deficits, and decreased economic activity even in Abu Dhabi, thus limiting the development funds available for the smaller emirates.

At the same time, the UAE suffered from a lack of coordination among the emirates on economic development. As al-Alkim explains, "Inter-emirate rivalries . . . impeded efforts to develop and industrialize on a federal rather than an individual basis."[16] As a result, emirates duplicated many facilities and services and competed among themselves for customers. For example, Abu Dhabi, Dubai, Sharjah, and Ras al-Khaimah all built international airports, but because there was only enough traffic to keep two of the airports busy, the facilities in Sharjah and Ras al-Khaimah were underused.

Despite its many economic problems, however, the UAE as a whole was successful not only at oil and gas production, but also at diversifying its economy to avoid total dependence on petroleum. Dubai led the way, becoming a center for both trade and manufacturing. Even before oil discoveries, Dubai's ruler at the time, Sheikh Maktoum, established that emirate as the gulf's gateway for imports to the region. By abolishing import and export tariffs, he encouraged merchants to resettle in and ship their products through Dubai, thereby creating a bustling trade economy. Later, Dubai developed industrial projects; for example, it became a major producer of aluminum at its Jebel Ali complex, using natural gas to produce the enormous amounts of energy needed to separate the metal from its ore. Dubai's success has been linked to its encouragement of foreign business investment by lifting restrictions on commerce in what are called free trade zones. Businesses in these locations can be 100 percent foreign owned, are not taxed, and the profits they earn need not stay within the UAE.

Although it relied more on its oil industry than Dubai did, Abu Dhabi also pursued nonoil development. It built plants to produce ammonia, sulfur, fertilizers, cement, iron, and steel, and developed mills to produce flour. In recent years, smaller emirates, too, have made some strides toward industrial development, using federal development funds. Sharjah, for example, began to manufacture large pipe used in oil pipelines, while Ajman fabricated steel and focused on ship repair, and Ras al-Khaimah developed its marble, limestone, and other quarries. These emirates, along with Umm al Qaywayn, also

Pictured is a skyscraper under construction along the Dubai waterfront. Dubai has long been the trade and manufacturing center of the UAE.

Dubai's busy port has contributed to the UAE's tremendous economic boom. Dubai remains the Persian Gulf's gateway for imported goods.

built cement factories. Fujairah, meanwhile, developed mining operations to extract various minerals found in its Hajar Mountains. In addition, all of the emirates increased their agricultural production and began to aggressively pursue the development of tourist industries.

Today, the UAE is experiencing an economic boom, its economy growing by almost 5 percent in 2003. A large part of the increase can be attributed to rising oil prices, but some growth also is still occurring in the nonoil sector of the economy, due to heavy private and public investments.

THE PERSIAN GULF WAR AND AMERICAN ALLIANCES

The UAE's economic growth has been helped by its successes in forming alliances with other countries, particularly its Arab neighbors. Its most important relationships are with other Persian Gulf states such as Saudi Arabia, Kuwait, Bahrain, Qatar, and Oman, with which it shares cultural traditions as well as economic and security interests.

The UAE and these five other gulf countries formalized their relationship in 1981 by creating the Gulf Cooperation Council (GCC).

The GCC grew out of security concerns raised by the Islamic revolution in Iran in 1979 and the outbreak of war between Iran and Iraq in 1980; the gulf states wanted to coordinate their defenses in case of an external military threat. However, its purpose also was to encourage cooperation among the six countries on economic matters. Since its inception, the GCC has made progress in both these areas. Steps have been taken to create a common currency and coordinate economic policy, and a GCC security cooperation agreement has been signed that commits the six nations to share security information in order to increase their ability to deal with domestic terrorist threats.

The Iraqi invasion of Kuwait in 1990, however, caused the UAE to rethink its strategy of relying only on other Arab states for protection. The UAE firmly backed Kuwait and cooperated closely with the United States when that nation led a UN military coalition to force Iraq to withdraw from Kuwait—a conflict that became known as the Persian Gulf War. The UAE began joint military exercises with the United States in July 1990, contributing more than $6 billion in aid during the war.

After the war, the UAE realized that it needed to arrange for similar superpower protection in the event that Iraq or some other country decided to attack it or take over its oil facilities. Accordingly, in 1992 the UAE signed an agreement with the United States that provided U.S. protection to the UAE and allowed the United States to use UAE air and naval bases. A more comprehensive Defense Cooperation Agreement calling for even closer military ties was signed two years later, on July 23, 1994. The UAE signed similar defense agreements with France and Britain. These relationships brought the UAE unambiguously into the Western sphere of influence in the Middle East.

As the new millennium approached, the UAE had grown stronger than ever before. In just three decades, it had managed to survive both internal and external threats, develop its economy into that of a modern nation, and acquire U.S. military protection. The young nation called the UAE clearly could be called a success.

4

TRADITION, RELIGION, AND CULTURE

Oil wealth has allowed the UAE to become a prosperous, highly developed country very rapidly. Indeed, even among other oil-producing countries in the region, few have managed such a transformation in only three decades. Yet despite the changes made possible by oil, the UAE continues to strongly reflect cultural and religious influences from its past.

TRADITIONAL ARAB CULTURE

The people of the modern state of the UAE, despite their recent affluence, remain faithful to their Arab traditions. For many people of the UAE, these traditions are comforting in the face of so much change; as scholar Frauke Heard-Bey has explained, "This is where the roots are, the strength and integrity of which enable people to respond to the radically changing life without losing their identity."[17]

Traditional Arab culture is largely based on Bedouin character and customs, which arose from trying to survive in the barren desert. Bedouin values important to survival in the desert included providing hospitality to all travelers, personal honor and dependability in the making of agreements, and bravery in battle. The desert environment also forced people to cooperate in order to survive. The result is a culture in which family and tribal loyalty is of vital importance. Families joined together to form clans, and clans combined to form tribes, which became the traditional Arab social and political unit. As Khalifa notes, tribes "provided [individuals] with a sense of identity and physical security against a characteristically hostile environment."[18]

Many of these traditional values and practices can be seen in action in the UAE today. As in many other Arab nations, people in the UAE are warm and hospitable, extremely loyal to their families, and protective of their personal reputations and honor.

The Tribal Political System

Within this tribal culture, political authority was given to a chief chosen by the elders. That decision was based on qualities such as leadership ability and embodiment of Bedouin values such as honesty and bravery. The ruler, however, exercised his authority only after consulting with others in the tribal leadership group—a practice called *shura*. Another tradition that arose from tribal rule was the *majlis*—the practice of the ruler meeting directly with his followers, allowing them to seek his help with problems or comment on his decisions. The two traditions created an essentially cooperative type of leadership in which tribal leaders, although not chosen directly by the people, made decisions

A group of Bedouin men relaxes in front of their tent with coffee and a hookah. The traditional Arab culture of the UAE is based largely on Bedouin customs.

only after seeking the input and assent of those they ruled. As the gulf states began to emerge, tribes began to cooperate in tribal confederations or fight with each other to conquer certain areas, with tribal leaders chosen from one family within the largest or most dominant tribe. Traditional tribal leadership evolved in this way into leadership of nations by several ruling families.

This tribal political tradition is still very evident in the UAE. The same families who ruled in the past continue to rule in the emirates today. For example, the Bani Yas tribal confederation still dominates Abu Dhabi; a separate branch of the Bani Yas rules Dubai; Sharjah and Ras al-Khaimah are ruled by Qawasim leaders; and other emirates are ruled by descendants of smaller tribes (Fujairah—Al-Sharqi; Umm al Qaywayn—Al-Ali; Ajman—Nuaim).

Although this tribal system has contributed to political stability, it has also kept the emirates divided. In the past, tribes often quarreled over issues such as grazing rights and water sources, and the modern emirates of the UAE continue to be divided by similar disputes over borders and power. Also, because people in the UAE continue to feel personal loyalty to the ruling sheikhs in each emirate, sometimes more than to the federal government, some observers say that many UAE citizens lack a strong sense of national citizenship. As historian J.B. Kelly has explained, "[A tribesman's] loyalty is personal to his tribe, his shaikh, or a leader of great consequence, and not to any abstract image of the state."[19]

THE IMPORTANCE OF ISLAM

Along with tribal loyalty, one of the strongest traditions in the UAE is respect for Islam and its moral teachings. Today, the overwhelming majority (about 96 percent) of the UAE's population is Muslim; only a few people practice other religions such as Christianity or Hinduism. For the Muslims of the UAE, as for Muslims everywhere, the essence of Islam is contained in what are called its "five pillars": (1) *shahada*, an affirmation of faith that must be recited daily ("There is no god but Allah, and Muhammad is his prophet"); (2) *salat*, prayer performed five times a day; (3) *zakat*, payment of a religious tax to benefit the poor; (4) *sawm*, fasting and refraining from smoking or having sex during the day for the month called Ramadan; and (5) going on the hajj, a pilgrim-

TRADITION, RELIGION, AND CULTURE

THE UAE'S SHARIA COURTS

In the UAE, there is a dual court system, with sharia (Islamic) courts that decide criminal and family law matters and nonreligious courts that decide all other matters. The civil courts are generally part of a federal court system, while each emirate administers its own sharia courts. In some emirates, however, in addition to family and criminal matters, these religious courts also decide all types of civil and commercial cases. In all courts, defendants have a right to legal counsel (but only after the police have finished their investigation), and cases are decided by judges, not juries. One of the religious penalties that sharia courts may impose (except in Dubai) is flogging—beating the convicted offender with a whip. Usually, this punishment is imposed on Muslims, and, in practice, it is done largely to shame the person and in a manner that prevents major or permanent injuries. Sharia penalties usually are not imposed on non-Muslims, but when they are they may be appealed to a higher court. Flogging sentences are commonly imposed in cases such as those involving prostitution, adultery, consumption of alcohol, or drug addiction. Other punishments, such as imprisonment, hanging, or stoning to death, can also be imposed by sharia courts, but death sentences are rare and must be personally approved by the UAE's president.

age to Mecca, which is considered the birthplace of Islam, once in one's lifetime. In addition, most of the UAE's Muslims (84 percent) are followers of one sect or branch of Islam called Sunni. These shared Sunni beliefs in the UAE create a high degree of homogeneity within its population and contribute not only to shared values, but also to relatively peaceful social relations in the country.

For most of the UAE's people, Islam is literally the most important element in their daily lives, and they take their religious duties very seriously. They stop whatever they are doing when it is time to say prayers, they typically give about 2.5 percent of their income to charity, and they arrange their work schedules in accordance with the dictates of Islam. In addition, Muslims in the UAE follow other Islamic practices, such as abstaining from eating pork and consuming alcohol, dressing modestly, and in general following a conservative lifestyle that places family at the forefront.

Muslim men kneel in prayer in a Dubai street. Life in the UAE revolves around the tenets of Islam.

The UAE's government does what it can to support these core Islamic values. In fact, Islam is designated in the UAE's constitution as the country's official religion. Also, Islamic law, called sharia, is the guiding force in the making of all laws and legislation, and religious judges, called *qadis*, use Islamic principles to make their decisions. Thus, most immoral behavior is illegal in the UAE and punishable under law. At the same time, Islam is generally tolerant of other religions, including Christianity. For this reason, the UAE's constitution provides freedom to worship for followers of all religions (as long as that practice does not conflict with government policy or violate accepted morals).

The trend toward a fundamentalist interpretation of Islam that has swept the Middle East since the early 1980s is reflected, in the UAE, in public behavior that is generally conservative. Unlike some nations in the region, however, the UAE has not experienced extremist behavior, such as the bombings that have been orchestrated by militant Islamic groups such as al Qaeda in Saudi Arabia. As Peck notes, "Despite the essentially conservative and pious attitudes of the general population, . . . extremism is shunned, and compromises are reached."[20]

TRADITIONAL DRESS

One sign of Emiratis' conservative nature is the fact that most wear traditional clothing designed to meet Islamic standards of modesty. The majority of men, for example, wear a long-sleeved, ankle-length robe called a *dishdasha*. The *dishdasha* covers the entire body but at the same time allows air to circulate; this helps cool the body during the heat of the day. In the summer, men usually wear a *dishdasha* made of white cotton to reflect sunlight, but in winter they usually choose a darker color and the garment is made from heavier, warmer fabrics such as wool. On their heads, men wear a traditional Arab covering made of three pieces: it starts with a cap that holds the hair in place (the *gahfiyya*), on top of which is worn a scarflike piece of cloth (the *ghutra*), which is held in place by a black cord (the *agal*). The headgear is very practical; it acts like an umbrella, providing protection from the sun, and the *ghutra* can be used to cover the mouth and the nose during sandstorms or cold weather. The entire head covering is often removed while indoors.

Emirati women in traditional dress make handicrafts in the shade of a tree. Most older Emirati women dress in traditional clothing.

The majority of Emirati women also dress conservatively. In public, most women wear a long, loose-fitting black garment called an *abaya* that, like the *dishdasha*, covers the whole body. It is usually worn with a black head cover (called a *shayla*) and sometimes with a veil (called a burka) that hides the face. Under the *abaya* or in private, women may wear a traditional Arabian dress known as a *kandura*, which also is full length and loose fitting, with long sleeves. The *kandura* often is made of silk and is sometimes very ornate, covered with elaborate beadwork or decorated by coins, sequins, or metal. On special occasions such as weddings, women may wear a *thoub*, a garment that is more finely designed than the *kandura*. Younger women also eagerly purchase Western clothes, and although some are bold enough to wear these clothes in public, others wear them only under the *abaya* or in private.

The UAE's adherence to tradition extends to Western visitors, who are expected to dress modestly. While the dress code in more urban areas such as Dubai is more relaxed, local laws in other parts of the country may go so far as to prohibit men from wearing shorts or appearing shirtless in public. Female visitors are advised not to wear shorts or skirts cut above the knee, tight or transparent clothing, or clothing that exposes their backs or stomachs. Even swimmers are expected to wear conservative swimwear, and should not wear swimsuits in the streets or other public places.

Family and Marriage Customs

One of the most revered institutions in the UAE's conservative society, and one that is unlikely to be subject to compromise, is the family. Traditionally, children and family form the heart of an Emirati's life and his or her strongest social bond. Most social activities take place in the context of the family. Families gather to enjoy meals, celebrate births and marriages, and simply spend time in each other's company. These family celebrations are kept extremely private and often held at home.

Families can be quite large, with two or more generations sharing a home. These families are traditionally organized under the leadership of the oldest male. Children are expected to be obedient to their elders. In the UAE, as in many Arab countries, the interests of the individual are less important than those of the family. All family members are therefore expected to avoid any behavior that might bring shame to the family.

Such expectations regarding behavior are particularly rigid when it comes to interactions between the sexes. Marriage is usually arranged by a young person's parents. As a result, in the UAE, there is no dating. Instead, parents and their marriage-age children discuss potential spouses, investigating their character and backgrounds, and then the father or mother approaches the other family to suggest a meeting. The young couple meets several times in a chaperoned group environment, and agrees either to proceed with the marriage or to part ways. These marriages often take place within the extended family, sometimes with cousins marrying one another. Indeed, traditionally the ideal match is considered to be between first cousins.

Traditional Poetry, Music, and Arts

Tradition also plays a central role in the cultural life of the UAE. A tradition of oral poetry and stories, for example, developed in the UAE as it did in other parts of the Arab world. This practice began with the Bedouin nomads, who often recited poetry and told stories, legends, folktales, proverbs, and parables in the evenings around fires in the desert. Indeed, because in the past most people could not read or write, each new generation learned about tribal history and ancestors, and the location of tribal territories, grazing areas, and oases, largely through this oral tradition rather than from written documents.

Later, poetry was written down and sometimes published in newspapers or books. One of the UAE's best-known early poets is Ibn Daher, who lived in Ras al-Khaimah in the seventeenth century. Today, poetry and stories are not as important to survival, but Emiratis continue to enjoy all forms of oral and written communications, and the UAE boasts many poets and novelists. Even UAE president Zayed is known for writing poetry.

A COFFEE SHOP SCENE IN DUBAI

The mixture of tradition and modernity in the UAE often results in a culture of contradictions, where old and new exist side by side, particularly in the more cosmopolitan cities such as Dubai. This is illustrated in a revealing passage from a book written by American professor Judith Caesar, called *Writing Off the Beaten Track:*

> I sat in a French-named coffee shop in an American-style shopping mall in Dubai drinking Italian espresso. A few tables away, a man in a *kandoora* [a traditional robe also called a *dishdasha*] was sipping coffee and speaking into a mobile phone. . . . Women in the traditional *abayahs* [traditional black robes] and *burqas* [traditional face coverings] stood veil to bare bicep with Eastern European tourists in miniskirts and halter tops, all looking at the same massive gold necklaces in the windows of the jewelry shops. Packs of teenage Arab girls, some in *abayahs* and *shillahs* [traditional scarves] some in skin-tight spandex and cropped tops, whispered and giggled. . . . Their male counterparts were sometimes in jeans, sometimes in *kandooras*, but in the latter case the traditional *ghutra* and *agal* [traditional head coverings for men] had been replaced by the ubiquitous backwards baseball cap.

Music and dance were another important part of Bedouin tradition, and so are part of life in the UAE. Typically, this traditional music features a variety of drums and other simple instruments such as an Arabian flute (the *mizmar*) and a string instrument (called *tamboura*). Musical performances are usually accompanied by traditional dances, the most popular of which are the *ayyalah*, which is a reenactment of a battle scene, the *liwa*, which was brought to the gulf by East African traders, and the *noban*, which has its origins in Nubia, a region of Egypt. Today in the UAE, groups of traditional folksingers, dancers, and musicians perform at almost every celebration; a sheikh's wedding, for example, will often include several troupes of musicians and dancers. The Internet site ArabNet describes the effect created by these performances:

> The music precedes the players, as the throb of drumbeats beckons through the twilight. A steadily increasing stream of people, attracted by the sound and the beat, move towards the gaily coloured lights, which mark the site of the celebration. The melody grows louder, the beat more insistent. Now it is not just the sound of one drum, but of several. The steady thumping of a bass drum is now overlaid with the higher

Emirati men perform traditional music and dance during a festival in Dubai. Music and dance are integral parts of life in the UAE.

pitched tattoo of smaller drums. As they come into view, the singers are accompanied by the wailing, treble melody of the flute. The dancers and singers are white-robed men, moving together slowly and rhythmically. Their voices rise and fall in a chorus as repetitive as the waves breaking on the sandy beaches of the Gulf shore. These entertainers may continue for half an hour or more without interruption, slowly dancing around in a circle, surrounded by a crowd of spectators. The musicians maintain their relentless rhythm, lending a totally hypnotic effect to the whole event.[21]

Other traditions include many decorative crafts. Islam generally frowns upon realistic depictions of humans or animals, so Islamic art often features fine calligraphy (a highly stylized type of handwriting) and colorful, intricate abstract or geometric patterns. These patterns are often found in decorative items such as rugs and wall hangings, which are popular for display in homes in the UAE. The government encourages the teaching of Islamic crafts in schools in order to preserve these traditions.

TRADITIONAL MARKETS

Another tradition that flourishes in the UAE is its markets, known as *souks*. In the past, souks were virtually the only place for people to shop for food and other essential goods. Modern souks in the UAE sell an even wider variety of merchandise, including food, spices, fabrics, plants, gold jewelry, rugs, electrical goods, car parts, and even camels. Despite the presence of Western-style shopping malls, the government has taken great care to preserve souks, which are often run as small family businesses. Today, as in the past, souks provide both a variety of goods as well as a meeting place where people gather to socialize or enjoy a cup of tea or Arabic coffee (called *gahwa*).

Typically, these modern souks are grouped together in one location and divided into areas selling similar items, so that shoppers can go to one spot to shop for food or whatever product they are interested in. In the souks, unlike Western-style malls or grocery stores, it is traditional for customers to bargain for the lowest price. Vendors expect that the first price they quote will be rejected and that the

customer will offer a lower price; this exchange continues until a final price is negotiated.

Perhaps the best-known UAE souks are those that specialize in gold. These are frequented by tourists as well as locals, because they offer some of the highest-quality gold jewelry in the world. Most of the jewelry made and sold in the UAE, for example, is solid gold and of the highest purity. Precious stones, pearls, and gold bars are also sold in the gold souks.

A customer haggles with a jewelry dealer in a Dubai souk. The gold jewelry sold in UAE's souks is of the highest quality.

CAMEL RACING, FALCONRY, AND ARABIAN HORSES

Shopping in the souks is a popular traditional pastime in the UAE, but the preservation of tradition can also be seen in sports such as camel racing, falconry, and racing of Arabian horses—all of which were part of Bedouin culture. The camel was essential to Bedouins, who relied on it for transportation and for carrying heavy loads across the desert. In addition, Bedouins relied on the camel for its milk, which is highly nutritious, and for its hair, which was woven into fabric for tents and blankets. The camel also provided entertainment in the form of racing, a tradition that has survived to modern times. During the winter months, usually in the

EMIRATIS' LOVE OF CAMELS

The Bedouin considered camels a gift from God. That is because camels were essential to desert life. First and foremost, they provided the Bedouin with a means of transportation. They could be ridden and raced like horses, or they could be loaded down with tents and belongings, or trade wares, for long caravans across the arid desert. However, camels also provided the Bedouin with answers to many of his other needs. Camel's milk was often the only source of protein available to desert families for months, and when necessary, a camel could be slaughtered to provide meat. Camel skin was used to make water containers, belts, and sandals; its dung was used as fuel; and its hair was woven into clothing, tents, and other items. Camels were also traded for essentials such as rifles, rice, coffee, sugar, and clothes.

Today, the people of the UAE no longer need the camel for transportation or food, but camels remain a beloved symbol of the country's Bedouin past. Many UAE families still own a few camels for milk and meat; this practice is subsidized by the government. Indeed, a recent survey found that one in every six UAE citizens in urban areas regularly drinks camel's milk, which has 40 percent less cholesterol and is higher in potassium, iron, and vitamin C than cow's milk. In addition, the ancient sport of camel racing still attracts enthusiastic crowds.

Modern-day Emiratis prepare for an early-morning camel race.

cooler morning hours, exciting races take place at modern racetracks throughout the country. The camels are ridden by very young boys, chosen because they weigh so little, who perch precariously on or behind the camel's hump. On special occasions, major races are held that pay hefty prizes, and Emiratis turn out in large numbers.

Even more popular than camels for racing are Arabian horses, which the Bedouin for generations bred for use both on long treks across the desert and on quick mounted raids against enemy camps. The result of such selective breeding is that Arabian horses have both speed and endurance. Horse-racing facilities and equestrian centers, used for pleasure riding, can be found in many major cities in the UAE. Dubai also hosts the Dubai World Cup, a racing event created in 1996 and held every March. Today it is one of the richest horse races in the world, paying prizes totaling $6 million and attracting competitors from around the globe.

Falconry is also a popular pastime throughout the gulf area. Like many of the UAE's traditions, it originated among the country's desert nomads, who used falcons to hunt game to supplement their otherwise meager desert diet of dates, milk, and bread. In modern times, the sport remains

Created in 1996, the Dubai World Cup is one of the world's richest horseracing events, attracting competitors from around the globe.

much the same: Wild falcons, birds of prey known for their beauty, loyalty, keen eyesight, and excellent hunting abilities, are trained to hunt other birds and small animals. The falcons are set loose by their trainers, known as *saggars*, to soar high in the sky. With their sharp eyesight, the falcons look for movement of prey on the ground; once prey is spotted, falcons dive downward at tremendous speeds and grab the prey with their sharp claws and beak. Trained falcons then bring the prey back to their handlers. Falcon hunting parties often travel to the desert, where they camp overnight and cook their game over open fires.

Yet another traditional sport is boat racing, including both sailboats and rowing competitions. The sailboats are modeled on boats that have been used by fisherman for centuries in the gulf, preserving yet another part of the country's past, when traders sailed from one port to another and fishermen put out to sea in search of fish to sell in local markets. Although oil wealth has brought many changes to the people of the UAE, they continue to take comfort and enjoyment from the traditions of their Bedouin past.

LIFE IN THE
MODERN UAE

Despite the continuing respect for religion and tradition, life has changed dramatically for the people of the UAE since the discovery of oil. For people who once lived a simple and isolated rural life, rapid development of the oil industry created an urban lifestyle filled with modern technology and bombarded by outside influences. Oil also eliminated poverty and provided the Emiratis, men and women alike, with benefits such as free education and government-paid health care. For many in the UAE, therefore, daily life is a privileged one in which most basic needs are met and time for leisure activities abounds.

AN URBAN SOCIETY

Just a generation ago, most people in the emirates had rural lifestyles, either roaming the deserts, fishing along the coast, or farming in small villages at oases or in the mountains. There were no roads connecting these villages and little communication with the outside world. Transportation on land was limited to camels or horses.

The discovery of oil, and the wealth it generated, changed all that, bringing the trappings of modern life. As Peck describes,

> Almost overnight the greater part of the population has been displaced from traditional rural (and/or maritime) modes of existence to a setting of artificially sustained vegetation, broad boulevards, luxury hotels, and replicated Wimpys, Seven-Elevens, and Burger Kings, where only a scattering of . . . huts might have been found a generation ago.[22]

65

Most Emiratis live in urban areas (pictured is a row of apartment buildings in Dubai) and enjoy many modern conveniences.

Today, most Emiratis live in these urban areas and have access to all sorts of modern conveniences. Village huts have been replaced by air-conditioned houses and high-rise apartment buildings. New luxury cars speed along newly built freeways and roads that lead to even the most remote parts of the UAE. Modern airports make it possible for Emiratis to fly to anywhere in the world. Telephones, televisions, and computers provide a constant link to other people, countries, and cultures.

HOUSING AND ARCHITECTURE

The most visible and immediate change made by oil revenues was in the housing and architecture of the UAE. Before the discovery of oil, many people lived in tents made from animal skins and hair during the winter and in shelters made of palm leaves during the summer. Permanent villages were small and primitive, consisting of huts or small houses constructed of whatever materials could be found nearby—mud and palm leaves near the coast and in oases, wood and stone in the mountains. To keep out the heat and to maintain privacy, windows were small and rarely opened onto the street. For ventilation, many houses also had wind towers, which were square and typically made of masonry;

they rose above the rooftop and were open on all sides to catch even the smallest breeze and funnel it into the rooms below.

Oil profits allowed the government to launch large construction projects to quickly upgrade the standard of living. It built public housing projects throughout the country, in which modern materials such as reinforced concrete and plaster supplanted mud and wood in the construction of homes. New mosques, schools, and health clinics were usually built at the same time. Yet modern houses in the UAE continue to incorporate traditional features. For example, houses are often divided into two parts: a reception area where guests are greeted and men sit and talk with one another, and a private area where women of the family congregate and where they are unlikely to be seen except by family members. Most houses have a decorative fence or wall for privacy and all are air-conditioned. Housing developments today are typically located on the outskirts of cities and are occupied by UAE citizens. Foreigners, by contrast, usually live close to city centers, in high-rise apartment buildings.

A TOURIST'S PARADISE

The UAE has earned a reputation as one of the best tourist destinations in the Arab world. There is a wide selection of accommodations, from economy to luxurious five-star hotels, and the country's pristine beaches, lush oases, undulating sand dunes, and rugged mountains provide a variety of scenic settings for tourists. There are also plenty of recreational, shopping, and sports opportunities to keep people entertained. Besides every type of water sport, horse and camel races, golf, and a new sport called sand surfing, travelers can shop at colorful souks (bazaars), visit old forts and fishing harbors, or encounter Arabic and Islamic architecture at magnificent mosques. Other attractions include safaris into the desert, trips to green oasis farms located in the midst of golden sand dunes, and excursions to the UAE's mountains. For those with a passion for history, the UAE has a number of archaeological sites, as well as museums that display ancient Arabic manuscripts and other treasures. Also, the people of UAE are known as friendly and hospitable to visitors; indeed, it is known as one of the safest spots in the Arab world.

Public buildings in the UAE, which house government ministries, corporate offices, and hotels, are often many stories tall and made of concrete, glass, and steel. In fact, some have compared the look of UAE cities to the city of Houston, Texas, because of their numerous sleek, modern-style skyscrapers. Some building styles are quite dramatic; for example, French architects and engineers designed the roof of the Armed Forces Officers' Club in Abu Dhabi to resemble the wings of a falcon.

EDUCATION, HEALTH CARE, AND SOCIAL PROGRAMS

For all UAE citizens, education, improved health care, and a range of new social benefits were perhaps the most welcome changes resulting from the new oil wealth. After the founding of the UAE, public education was given top priority by the government. The education system was generously funded and dramatically expanded, resulting in an increase in the number of people who can read and write from just a few to almost 80 percent of the population in 2003.

Emirati schoolchildren enjoy a field trip to a museum. Education is a top priority in the UAE.

Today, education in the UAE includes twelve years of compulsory schooling. In addition, the country provides university-level postsecondary schooling at several institutions, including the United Arab Emirates University. All education, from primary level to university, is free at government-run schools. There are also private schools, attended by about 40 percent of the student population. Many of these schools provide education to the various communities of foreigners living in the UAE, in their native language and using curricula from their home countries; other schools focus on Arab and Islamic studies. In addition, generous government grants are provided for those who want to study abroad. Although compulsory for all children, education in the UAE is largely segregated by gender except for kindergarten and the lower primary grades. These separate facilities are meant to accommodate the desires of conservative UAE families who interpret Islam as prohibiting unrelated men and women from having close contact with each other, even in heavily monitored environments such as classrooms.

Just as the government provides its citizens with schooling, so, too, does it provide a modern health-care system with facilities and professionals capable of giving excellent care. In addition, the UAE provides extensive social welfare benefits that include family care aimed at solving domestic problems and psychological treatment centers for troubled youths, as well as housing and benefits to widows, orphans, the elderly, the disabled, and others unable to support themselves. These benefits were once free to all UAE residents, but the government has recently begun charging noncitizens for health care and other services.

WORK AND INCOME

In addition to providing comprehensive education and social benefits, the UAE government is the nation's largest employer and reserves for its citizens the most senior and highest-paid jobs. Most native Emiratis today work directly for the government or in government-related industries and organizations. These include not only government agencies and the oil industry, but also other companies owned by the government, such as manufacturers, banks, and real estate concerns. Most citizens work as managers, bureaucrats, or in other prestigious positions. They generally do not hold jobs that require manual labor, long hours, or low pay; instead, foreigners are hired for these types of jobs in industries such as oil, construction, fishing, household labor, retail stores, and hospitality (restaurants and hotels).

This availability of education, social benefits, and high-paid work means that the people of the UAE can afford one of the highest standards of living in the world. Although some Emiratis are quite rich, most live in a way that would be considered very comfortable by people in the United States. They own houses, drive nice cars, and have money to spend on possessions such as clothes, TVs, cell phones, electronic equipment, leisure activities, and vacations. However, a combination of factors is creating a high rate of unemployment among UAE citizens and threatening their prosperity. Rapid population growth and the availability of cheap foreign labor has put a strain on the government's ability to provide for its citizens, especially during periods when oil prices (and income) drop. In addition, a large number of young, educated Emiratis enter the workforce every year, putting pressure on the government to provide more good jobs; in 2010, for example, about ninety-three thousand young men are expected to reach working age. The country hopes to find ways to absorb this new generation into the workforce; otherwise, these Emiratis may depend even more on social benefits provided by the government.

FOREIGN WORKERS/RESIDENTS

The legions of foreign workers who fill the jobs Emiratis do not want give parts of the UAE a very cosmopolitan flavor. Foreign residents bring with them their native foods, languages, and customs. Because the foreign population vastly exceeds that of Emiratis, however, some say that parts of the UAE are beginning to lose their Arab flavor: Referring to the large number of mostly Asian foreign workers in Dubai, analyst Anthony H. Cordesman calls the UAE "the most successful Asian nation in the Gulf."[23]

This foreign population lives in a world separate from that of UAE citizens. Typically, they are eager to work in the UAE because they are poor and come from countries that offer few opportunities. Most receive from their employers housing or housing allowances, access to medical care, and payment of their travel expenses home. Although some are

relatively well paid, working as teachers, doctors, and administrators, many foreign workers work in manual, unskilled jobs and do not earn very much. They are often employed, for example, as construction workers, as laborers at oil facilities, or as household help. Indeed, most foreign workers do not even earn the $1,090 per month minimum salary the government requires before they are allowed to bring their families to the UAE.

Despite their low pay, foreign workers generally do not complain and do not report mistreatment out of fear that their employers will fire them or have them deported. Yet the government is concerned that foreign workers may at some point begin to resent native Emiratis and their access to better jobs, pay, and benefits. Social turmoil could result and present the government with a dilemma: Although the government could deport foreigners who make trouble, that would leave the country without the workers necessary to run its industries and economy.

In the UAE, foreign workers like these Indians cleaning fish in a Dubai souk work in low-paying, menial jobs.

WOMEN IN THE UAE

One possible source of workers that the UAE is tapping into is women who want to work outside the home. In fact, oil discoveries have created a vast improvement in the status of women in the UAE, and although many women still lead very traditional lives as wives and mothers, female citizens as a group have pursued new opportunities for education and work. When the UAE offered universal education, for example, women flocked to schools and universities. Indeed, the number of female students registered at UAE schools has increased dramatically since the 1970s; approximately 270,000 female students were registered in 1996–1997, compared with only 19,000 in 1972–1973. In higher education, women now make up the majority of the UAE's students. As reporter Habeeb Salloum describes, "Through education, under a . . . government whose priority has always been women's issues, women in the UAE have literally blossomed, achieving the highest rate of development in the Arab countries."[24]

This education has given women much greater access to jobs once available only to male citizens. Today, for example, women constitute 20 percent of the UAE labor force and hold senior positions throughout the economy—mostly in the government, particularly in the education and health ministries, but also in some private companies. Women, for example, work in fields as diverse as architecture, banking, cosmetics, engineering, insurance, and the media. Many UAE women are even joining police forces and the military, careers that were once unthinkable for women in any Arab country.

Although the UAE's constitution and laws provide for such equal opportunities for women, these accomplishments for women have resulted largely from the efforts of Sheikha Fatima bin Mubarak, Sheikh Zayed's wife and the UAE's first lady. Fatima in 1975 founded the UAE Women's Federation, a government-funded body that has strongly promoted women's education and woman's rights in the UAE. The Women's Federation acts as an advocate for women with government ministries, and its thirty-one local offices offer a wide variety of classes and provide services such as child care advice, health education, vocational training, job placement programs, and family mediation services. Both Fatima and her husband believe that the UAE's society will reap great benefits from bringing women into all walks of life. In fact, one of Fatima's current campaigns is for the women of the UAE to move into the political arena and become members of the country's parliamentary assembly, the Federal National Council.

The UAE's support of woman's rights is viewed by some outsiders as surprising, given the conservative nature of traditional Islamic societies, which out of concern for morality and respectability often seclude women from society and prevent them from working or socializing with men. In the more conservative neighboring country of Saudi Arabia, for example, Muslim women have many fewer opportunities. The leaders of the UAE, however, see empowerment of women as consistent with the teachings of Islam. As Zayed has explained, "These eternal values [of Islam and Arab traditions] reject the humiliation of the woman and call for her honouring and giving her all her rights."[25]

SHEIKHA FATIMA BIN MUBARAK

Sheikha Fatima bin Mubarak, wife of UAE president Sheikh Zayed, is a heroine for many women in the UAE and throughout the Middle East. With her husband's support, she has worked since the time of the UAE's independence to improve the lives of the country's women. In 1972 Fatima founded the first women's society, the Abu Dhabi Women's Society, which led in August 1975 to the establishment of the UAE Women's Federation, a national body with its own budget to assist UAE women.

The federation's goal in the early days was to help women come out of the seclusion imposed by traditional culture, learn to read and write, and become knowledgeable about the modern world, as a means of raising their families' standards of living. Since then, the federation has successfully encouraged women to compete at all levels of education and in the workplace. Fatima emphasizes that women can be participants in society while at the same time continuing their traditional motherhood roles and adherence to the teachings of Islam. For example, she supported a 1999 maternity leave law that provides working women three months of leave at full pay and six more months at half pay to take care of their newborns. Fatima has received numerous awards for her leadership in woman's rights, including the United Nations (UN) Shield in 1986 from the UN Population Fund, various UN recognition awards in 1997, and the Humanitarian Personality of the Year award for 1998 in Dubai.

TRANSPORTATION, COMMUNICATIONS, AND THE MEDIA

Other changes wrought by oil prosperity in the UAE include new transportation systems, as well as advanced telephones, radio, and television, and a proliferation of newspapers. Road building was given a high priority in the 1970s because good transportation was seen as crucial to the nation's development. At the time the country was founded, there were only three highways connecting Abu Dhabi, Dubai, and Sharjah. A decade later, the UAE had succeeded in constructing a nationwide system of highways linking all of the emirates.

Today in the UAE, most residents travel by car, in numbers large enough to create occasional traffic congestion. Dubai, however, operates a public bus system and is planning to build an automated train system. The UAE also has several major international airports—in Abu Dhabi, Dubai, Ras al-Khaimah, and Sharjah. Airports in Abu Dhabi, Dubai, and Ras al-Khaimah specialize in passenger service, while Sharjah is renowned for its commercial cargo facilities. Finally, Abu Dhabi, Dubai, and Sharjah have built a number of the finest seaports in the world; they are used largely for commercial shipping activities.

A Dubai man talks on his cell phone. The UAE has one of the highest rates of cell phone usage in the Middle East.

INTERNET ACCESS IN THE UAE

The UAE reportedly has more Internet users than any other country in the Arab world. The country has many cybercafés, where people can use the Internet for a small fee, and the Internet is also accessible in people's homes. However, according to Human Rights Watch, a group that monitors these issues, the UAE at the same time has led the region in advocating for censorship of the Web. As a result, Internet users in the UAE do not access the Internet directly. Instead, they dial in to a server maintained by Etisalat, the country's Internet provider, which refuses access if the URL requested is on a list of banned sites or if a content check of the site shows objectionable material. The government's main objective is to block access to sexually explicit and porno-graphic sites, particularly to children; it maintains that there is no restriction of political, social, or economic materials. However, Human Rights Watch discovered that the UAE also blocks access to some cultural and political sites as well.

Two men in traditional dress access the Internet in a Dubai cybercafe.

The UAE's transportation system is matched by an equally modern communications system, which the UAE claims is the most advanced in the gulf. It is run by the Emirates Telecommunications Corporation, a company owned by the government, and provides nationwide telephone service of nine hundred thousand lines with direct dialing to 246 countries. Mobile phone service is also available, and the

An Emirati reads a newspaper account of Saddam Hussein's capture. The government is somewhat restrictive of what the press may publish.

UAE has one of the highest cell phone usage rates in the Middle East, due mostly to low subscription fees. Similarly, the UAE has the highest rate of Internet use in the Middle East region because access is cheap and it is available in people's homes. Finally, the UAE has developed lively mass media, including numerous newspapers as well as radio and television stations that broadcast a variety of entertainment and news programs in English, Arabic, and other languages. Television viewers can choose from government-run local stations and a number of satellite networks such as the British Broadcasting Corporation (BBC), Arabic news network Al-Jazeera, CNBC, and Showtime.

Although the UAE has a reputation for greater press freedom than many other nations in the Middle East, it still restricts journalists from criticizing the government, the ruling families, or friendly foreign governments. All newspapers, for example, are given instructions by the government about what news may be covered. In addition, the Ministry of Information must license all publications and approve the appointment of editors. As a result of these strict controls, journalists in the UAE rarely publish challenging, investigative articles about local politics or government policies. Also, the UAE government uses filtering technology to block access to sexually explicit and politically sensitive Internet sites.

On the other hand, foreign journalists are often subject to fewer government controls than their domestic colleagues. For example, the news broadcasting company Cable News Network (CNN) cited press freedom as a reason for picking Dubai in 2002 as the location for its Arabic-language Web site and news bureau. As Ronald Ciccone, senior vice president and managing director of CNN Middle East, explained, "CNN picked Dubai as its news gathering centre because of its strategic position, the worldwide reputation it enjoys and the freedom of the press it guarantees."[26]

FOOD AND DINING

The new wealth created by oil also has allowed the people of the UAE to indulge even more often in one of their most cherished rituals—dining on good food. Indeed, food is one of the delights in the UAE, where traditional spicy Middle Eastern fare is the norm, but where one can also find a variety of foods from the West and other parts of the world.

A typical traditional meal starts with appetizers such as stuffed vine leaves, tabouleh (chopped parsley, mint, and crushed wheat), or hummus (a paste made from chickpeas, garlic, and sesame seeds spread on Arab flat bread). The main course usually includes dishes made from chicken, lamb, or fish, heavily spiced and served with rice. Fresh seafood from the Persian Gulf, such as lobster, crab, shrimp, grouper, tuna, kingfish, or red snapper, is often featured. Other popular traditional ingredients are goat cheese (feta), eggs, salad, olives, honey, fruit, almonds, and dates. After dinner, sweet desserts such as *lugaimat* and *khanfaroosh* (similar to doughnuts, with honey or date syrup) are offered, along with either tea or coffee flavored with a spice called cardamom.

In the cities, however, restaurants and stores catering to tourists and the large population of foreign workers make a wide variety of foreign foods easily available. Almost any type of food, such as Italian, French, Mexican, Polynesian, Japanese, Chinese, Thai, Korean, Indian, Pakistani, and Persian, can be found. These foods are served at some of the finest restaurants in the Middle East as well as in small local ethnic cafés. The UAE also has international fast-food chains (such as McDonald's, Pizza Hut, Dunkin' Donuts, and KFC), and American theme restaurants (such as T.G.I. Friday's).

These restaurants are often frequented by visitors and foreign workers, but also sometimes by Emiratis.

Because Muslims are prohibited from eating pork, however, it is never served as part of traditional meals and is not included in menus at restaurants that Emiratis are likely to patronize. At some resorts or hotels with largely international clienteles, pork might be served, but menus clearly label dishes that include pork to help Muslims avoid eating it. Like pork, alcohol is also prohibited for Muslims; it, too, is sold only in hotel restaurants and bars. Restaurants outside of these hotels cannot legally serve alcohol.

SPORTS AND LEISURE

Soccer is the UAE's most popular team sport. Here, a player with the UAE team (left) struggles with a member of the Bahrain team for control of the ball.

In addition to good food, people living in UAE today look to sports and popular entertainment for recreation and relaxation. In fact, Emiratis watch or participate in sports that were virtually unheard of before oil brought wealth—and foreign influences—to the country. For example, team sports, a uniquely Western idea, are very popular in the

UAE. Probably the most popular team sport is football (known as soccer in the United States). The sport is played at schools and universities and all the emirates have soccer stadiums, including Zayed Sports City in Abu Dhabi, the largest sports complex in the Middle East.

Other sports activities include cricket, a game popular among the UAE's large Indian population, and golf, which is growing in popularity. The country has built many golf courses, at least three of which are PGA championship courses, and Dubai hosts the Dubai Desert Classic, a golf event featuring some of the world's best golfers, who compete for over $1 million in prizes. The UAE also hosts a car rally called the Desert Challenge, and Emiratis enjoy water sports such as swimming, windsurfing, waterskiing, scuba diving, fishing, yacht racing, and powerboat competitions.

Other leisure attractions include theater and films. For tourists, expeditions into the desert, visits to oasis farms, and excursions to the mountains are available. Indeed, because of its range of activities, beauty, and tolerance for other cultures, the UAE has become a very popular tourist destination. Tourists have discovered what Emiratis have known since the nation's founding—that the UAE is a place of wealth, luxury, and leisure.

6

CHALLENGES AHEAD

The UAE has developed rapidly since its discovery of oil, transforming a poor desert land into a modern, developed nation virtually overnight. However, the country's most difficult challenges may lie ahead, given the advanced age of its president, simmering disagreements among the emirates, newly arising social and economic problems, and potential security threats in an increasingly volatile Middle East.

AFTER SHEIKH ZAYED

As the UAE looks to the future, the fact that it has more than a hundred years' worth of oil and gas reserves means it likely can afford to support its citizens' comfortable lifestyle for some time. Yet the future is also expected to present daunting challenges. One of the greatest of these is finding someone to rule the country after its president, Sheikh Zayed bin Sultan al-Nuhayyan, now approaching ninety years old and in failing health, dies or steps down.

Zayed has been widely praised by both Emiratis and leaders of other countries for his wise and patient leadership. Most observers say he is largely responsible for the UAE's success in developing into a modern nation. As professor Eesa Mohammed Bastaki explains,

> [Zayed] enjoys, and deserves, the confidence of fellow rulers and citizens alike, for since the [UAE] was established, it has successfully passed through an utter transformation from a backward country to one of the fastest developing in the world, and has done so without the accompanying social, political and economic

disruption that has marred the development process in so many other countries.[27]

Observers point out that Zayed has been particularly good at resolving disputes between the emirates and promoting cooperation among them. Many people wonder whether Zayed's replacement can provide the same strong leadership for the UAE in future years.

Zayed's plan is for his eldest son, Crown Prince Sheikh Khalifa bin Zayed, to succeed him as ruler of Abu Dhabi. Presumably, Khalifa would also become president of the UAE, although this is not certain, since under the UAE constitution the ruler of any emirate could theoretically be chosen as president as long as that choice is agreed to by both Dubai and Abu Dhabi. In any case, Khalifa has been working to prepare himself to head the UAE's government. He already holds the position of deputy supreme commander of the UAE Armed Forces. Also, in recent years he has represented his father at international gatherings, such as meetings of the GCC states, in addition to handling much of the UAE's day-to-day business. However, Khalifa has his own health problems: He already has had one stroke.

THE UAE AND TERRORISM

After the terrorist attacks on the United States on September 11, 2001, UAE president Sheikh Zayed quickly sympathized with the United States and condemned the terror strikes. Since then, the UAE has fully cooperated with the United States in its war against terrorism. For example, when it was discovered that money was transferred to Mohammed Atta, the leader of the September 11 hijackers, through Dubai using the *hawala* method (an informal banking system that works outside traditional banking and financial channels), the UAE acted quickly. It provided intelligence on these transactions and tightened regulations to make it harder for fundamentalist Islamic groups to transfer funds through UAE in the future. Also, the UAE's security services worked with the CIA and the FBI to locate and extradite people involved in the financing of al Qaeda terror activities. This effort has been successful: Several have been arrested, including Abdel Rahim al-Nashiri, a senior al Qaeda figure who was believed to be planning terror strikes against major economic targets in the UAE.

Zayed's other sons also hold important posts in the emirate of Abu Dhabi, the federal government, or both. Zayed's second son, Sheikh Sultan, was UAE deputy prime minister and minster of state for foreign affairs until 2003, when Zayed replaced him with his fourth son, Sheikh Hamdan. Zayed's third son, Sheikh Muhammad, is chief of staff of the UAE Armed Forces. All are reported to be quietly jockeying for power should Khalifa not become the next leader.

Observers also note that there remains a possibility of open rivalry between the seven emirates over the succession issue. Before independence, the emirates that formed the UAE frequently experienced coups and struggles over power. Also, as recently as 2003, another emirate, Ras al-Khaimah, witnessed gunfire and street protests following a decision by its aged ruler, Sheikh Saqr bin Mohammed al-Qassimi, to demote his eldest son, Sheikh Khalid, and appoint his fourth son, Sheikh Saud, as crown prince and successor. Saqr apparently began to worry about Khalid's views on certain matters, including his anti-U.S. attitudes.

Crown Prince Sheikh Khalifa bin Zayed, shown here greeting British prime minister Tony Blair in 2003, is expected to succeed Sheikh Zayed as leader of the UAE.

Khalid publicly complained about the decision, encouraging people to protest; order was restored in Ras al-Khaimah only after Abu Dhabi sent armored vehicles to put down the uprising. Those who follow politics in the region say that this type of rivalry at the national level could lead to political instability for the UAE.

Some analysts, however, say fears surrounding Zayed's succession may be misplaced. For example, similar worries about succession in the UAE's second-largest emirate, Dubai, proved unfounded when, following Rashid's death in 1990, rivalries among his sons were quickly worked out. The eldest son, Maktum, became ruler; the second-eldest, Hamdan, became deputy ruler; and the third-eldest, Muhammad, was named heir apparent. Analysts say this type of arrangement might serve as a model for how a smooth succession might be arranged for the UAE's central leadership.

PROBLEMS OF FEDERATION DISUNITY

Still, questions about future UAE leadership sharpen historical divisions among the emirates. Although Zayed has been able to hold the seven emirates together through negotiation and compromise, some observers worry that the individual emirates' tendency to proceed independently on policy matters that affect their interests will work against national interests. For example, many institutions that are run by the federal government in most countries, such as the military and economic development programs, are still largely controlled by individual emirates in the UAE. As Cordesman notes, "The UAE has not developed strong unifying institutions that unite the Emirates at levels below the royal families." [28]

The emirates also often disagree about issues of foreign policy—typically a federal concern. The emirate of Ras al-Khaimah, for example, continues to hold a grudge against the neighboring country of Oman following an open confrontation in 1977 over the border, even though the other emirates want improved relations with Oman. Other differences between the emirates have arisen in their policies toward Iran and Iraq. For example, Abu Dhabi supported Iraq during the Iran-Iraq War, while Dubai and Sharjah were more inclined toward Iran. In 1992, Iran's reassertion of full control over islands belonging to Sharjah and Ras al-Khaimah (after sharing control for many years) led to another mixed response, with the UAE officially opposing Iran's actions even as Dubai and Sharjah continued economic ties to Iran. The UAE exhibited a similar ambiguous attitude toward Iraq. Although the UAE backed Kuwait after Iraq's 1990 invasion, the emirates differed on issues such as trade sanctions against Iraq during the 1990s.

ECONOMIC REFORMS

Another area that analysts say requires attention in the future is the UAE's economy. The country's future security, they say, may depend on how it manages the wealth its oil and gas generate.

Above all, experts say, the UAE must decide how to share its oil revenues fairly among the seven emirates when only one of the emirates, Abu Dhabi, owns most of its oil and gas reserves. The current system—in which Abu Dhabi keeps most of its oil income but contributes to a federal budget that largely funds the smaller emirates—still leaves people in the five smaller emirates much poorer than citizens of Abu Dhabi and Dubai. In 1993, for example, the per capita income of Abu Dhabi was $20,664, while the per capita income of Ajman—the smallest and poorest emirate—was $4,257. These disparities naturally contribute to jealousy and division and distract the emirates from addressing their common economic and security concerns.

Other economic issues concern the need to reduce the nation's reliance on its oil industry. Currently, the UAE's economy is vulnerable to fluctuations in oil prices. Furthermore, economists say the UAE needs a source of income after its oil is depleted. In fact, the UAE has had more success in this area than most other nations in the region. It has invested heavily in nonoil industries and its nonoil income has grown steadily since the 1970s. However, some analysts say that much of the nonoil activity has been in short-term construction projects and in trade, both of which depend on imports and will be harmed if the nation's oil income drops. Economists say, therefore, that the UAE must work to become truly economically diverse and independent.

Some experts see a solution in selling government-owned businesses to private investors, a process known as privatization. This, it is claimed, would lead to more development

of nonoil industries and produce more efficiency and productivity in the UAE's economy. In addition, the UAE is being urged by experts to increase the opportunities for foreign investment. These experts suggest that other emirates follow Dubai's lead in creating free-trade zones to attract foreign investors; other experts suggest lifting restrictions on foreign investment outside these zones to further encourage international trade and bring new nonoil industries to the UAE.

Although oil rigs like this one continue to supply the UAE with profitable oil reserves, the government is working to diversify the nation's economy.

THE FOREIGN WORKER PROBLEM

Perhaps the most worrisome feature of the UAE economy is its dependence on foreign workers. In addition to social and labor unrest that could develop due to the wide difference in living standards between foreigners and citizens, the UAE government has other fears. For example, some argue that the influx of outsiders who do not share Emiratis' customs, religion, and traditions has contributed to a dilution of Arab culture and a rise in social problems such as crime and drug

The UAE's economy depends on foreign workers like these Indians, whose growing influence may affect the nation's future.

abuse. Also, the government fears that Islamic fundamentalists from countries such as Iran might sow unrest among Emiratis with similar beliefs, leading to a revolution similar to the one that shook Iran in 1979.

Another government concern is the drain on resources caused by providing housing, health care, and other resources to a large number of noncitizens. The large number of foreigners, many of whom are illegal immigrants, are helping to swell the population of the UAE. The United Nations estimates that the UAE's population will double by 2018. Such an increase will place great stress on the government's ability to continue providing a high standard of living for its people. In addition, the rapid increase in population is depleting the country's water supplies. Although desalinization (removing the salt from seawater) and recycling help provide water for some of the UAE's needs and stretches supplies, it is expected that the country will exhaust its groundwater reserves in only twenty to fifty years.

To combat these problems, the government has taken several steps. To reduce the political and population risks, the government has sought to substitute laborers from Asia for those from other Arab nations. Workers from nations such as Korea and the Philippines rarely seek to settle permanently in the UAE and tend not to bring their families, reducing the chances that they will add to population growth. Because they are generally not Muslims, they also do not pose the political risk of workers from Arab countries.

To save money, the government has cut back on the benefits provided to foreigners. For example, in 1983 it stopped providing free medical care to foreigners, except those who work for the federal government, and since then it has imposed higher taxes, water and electricity prices, and visa fees on foreigners. To maintain security, the government exercises tight control on foreigners by deporting anyone who engages in labor disputes, aggressively arresting and deporting illegal immigrants, and permanently banning workers who violate their work contracts by engaging in criminal or other prohibited activities.

However, analysts doubt these steps by the UAE's government are sufficient. As Cordesman notes, "It is extremely doubtful that the UAE can maintain a stable society, or suitable per capita earnings, without more drastic measures to cut its reliance on foreign labor."[29] The government is aware of this and is considering more aggressive actions to reduce the number of foreign workers and increase the number of citizens in the labor force—a process known as emiratization. Among the steps being looked at are changes in school curricula so that citizens can acquire the skills they need to replace foreign workers. The government is also considering making changes to UAE's laws, which now penalize companies for hiring UAE citizens by requiring that these employees receive higher wages, more benefits, and greater job security than foreign workers get.

Economic experts also have urged the UAE to scale back its generous social benefits, in order to give citizens the incentive to take less desirable jobs now held by foreigners. They point out that the UAE's generosity—its hiring of citizens for high-paid, undemanding government jobs, lack of taxation, and provision of health and social benefits—is destroying Emiratis' work ethic. Indeed, many of the children of the UAE's wealthiest families are choosing not to work, a development that caused Zayed to speak out strongly on the value of work in a series of major speeches in the 1990s. On one occasion, for example, he implored, "Youth unemployment is unacceptable. . . . Young people should work, and earn through their sweat, so that they become an example for their sons and brothers. A healthy person who does not work commits a crime both against himself and against his country."[30] Cutting benefits, however, will be a politically difficult step for the government to take after so many years of generosity. Despite the fact that Emiratis do not vote, observers note that they could express their displeasure in *majlis* meetings or even threaten the government with street protests.

SOCIAL CONCERNS

Yet another challenge for UAE society will be maintaining its careful balance between modernization and openness and its conservative culture and values. Although many praise the country for achieving such balance in the past, a new generation of Emiratis will soon emerge whose experiences are more in the modern world and less rooted in tradition.

Young women, in particular, can be expected to continue their quest for education and work opportunities not available to their mothers, a development that is already changing traditional family and social patterns. Many women, for example, now postpone marriage until after they finish college, reversing the tradition of women marrying at very young ages, often to older men. Also, although many women still do not enter the workforce after earning their degrees, often because of their husband's or family's opposition, an increasing number choose to work outside the home, sometimes alongside men—a practice that would have been taboo in the past.

The changes that have allowed women to work have also led to the need for child care arrangements in which children are raised by nannies, who are often non-Arab and are therefore unable to train them in traditional or religious values. Another development is a high rate of marriages between UAE males and non-Arab foreign women, which leave many UAE children to be raised by mothers with absolutely no cultural or religious ties to the country. Many worry that these trends will be detrimental for families, the backbone of the UAE's social order.

Authorities are already concerned about what they see as signs of a weakening of the social order. They cite increasing rates of divorce, crime, violence against women, child abuse, and drug addiction, all of which were uncommon until recent times. Some blame these problems on the presence of so many foreign workers, who are seen as morally lax compared to people who grew up with traditional Muslim values. Others contend that the problems are part of modern-day life, the result of people being exposed to a

A Bedouin Emirati weaves thread on a loom. The government promotes handicrafts as part of an effort to keep traditional practices alive.

wider variety of stresses and temptations than would be the case in a closed, traditional society.

The government has sought to cope with these problems by promoting traditional customs and values. One example is the Marriage Fund, which encourages marriage among UAE citizens by providing loans to men wishing to marry Emirati women, helping the couple to get a good start in life. The government also provides other services, such as long maternity leaves, family counseling, and religious education, in order to support families and traditional values. To further preserve Emirati culture, the government also promotes activities such as traditional handicrafts, sports, and architecture. Whether these efforts can maintain the UAE's essentially Arab and Islamic character remains to be seen.

FOREIGN POLICY

Finally, the UAE will be challenged in the future to maintain its security amid unstable and potentially aggressive neighbors in the Middle East. One danger involves the UAE's continuing troubles with Iran. As recently as the 1990s, for example, the dispute over Iran's takeover of Abu Musa and the Tunb islands resurfaced. Following its 1971 seizure of the islands, Iran constructed military facilities on Abu Musa but allowed some Emiratis to remain on the island. In March 1992 Iran, claiming it had not received its share of the island's oil production, suddenly reasserted control of the island and expelled everyone who was not Iranian. The crisis continued for years as Syria and other countries tried to mediate, but today the stalemate lingers: Iran still occupies the islands, and the UAE continues to assert sovereignty over them.

In the 1990s the UAE had a territorial dispute with another neighboring country, Qatar. The disagreement concerned historical claims by both countries to Khaur al-Udaid, an inlet on the eastern side of the Qatari peninsula

FOREIGN AID

The UAE, in keeping with Islamic principles of helping the less fortunate, has been a generous donor, particularly to Arab and Islamic countries. Over the years, for example, the UAE has had great sympathy for the Palestinian people and their struggle with Israel over the creation of a Palestinian state. To show its support, the UAE has regularly channeled financial support to the Palestinians, primarily to more moderate groups led by Palestinian leader Yasir Arafat. The UAE also provides significant aid to non-Arab Islamic countries. Its ties to both Pakistan and India are especially close, due to the large numbers of foreign workers from those countries. In 2001, for example, the UAE granted Pakistan a package of development loans totaling over $265 million, the largest single package of assistance ever awarded by the country's development fund.

In addition, the UAE is a large source of international humanitarian aid. Its Red Crescent Society (RCS), the equivalent of the Red Cross, ranks first among Arab charity organizations and is known as one of the world's best emergency assistance societies. In the year 2000 alone the RCS spent $34.4 million on relief activities, largely in areas such as Palestine, Kosovo, Pakistan, and Afghanistan. Another UAE humanitarian group, the Zayed Foundation, also extends significant humanitarian aid. Indeed, it was recognized by the United Nations in 2000 as fifth among all bodies worldwide providing relief for refugees. The UAE also was one of the first countries to provide aid to Iraqis following the U.S. invasion in 2003.

and the territory behind it. Many believed that the issue had been settled years earlier by negotiations conducted by Zayed, but in 1995 and 1996 relations deteriorated again when Qatar accused the UAE of supporting an unsuccessful coup. Tensions eventually eased but relations between the two countries continue to be rocky.

In addition, the UAE is concerned about regional instability caused by the ongoing instability in Iraq. After the United States invaded and overthrew the government of Saddam Hussein in 2003, UAE leaders hoped that good relations could be established with a new, stable Iraqi government. UAE firms benefited from Iraq reconstruction contracts and, with U.S. encouragement, the UAE was preparing for increased trade with Iraq. However, for the UAE and other Middle East nations, continuing violence and the possibility of a civil war in Iraq have created new security concerns. The worry is that the violence could spread beyond Iraq's borders or that the government that eventually emerges in Iraq might be hostile to the UAE.

To prepare its defenses against these types of regional threats, the UAE has increased its military budget in the last several decades. In 1978, for example, the UAE's total military expenditures were only about $822 million, but by 1991, they had increased to $4.9 billion. However, despite the unification of armed forces into a national military force in 1976, the command of military forces has largely stayed with the individual emirates and there has been little centralization of arms purchases or military training. In addition, although the country has an army that numbers about sixty-five thousand men run by an officers' corps staffed largely by UAE citizens, many of its foot soldiers are foreigners from other Arab countries, which the UAE hires to fill out the limited pool of UAE citizens available for military service. To remedy these problems, military analysts urge the UAE to make decisions about military expenditures and other issues at the national level, based on what is good for the country overall, and to seek better coordination of military policy among the individual emirates.

Even with reforms, however, experts say the UAE's military, for the foreseeable future, will not be capable of defending the country without help from neighboring countries and Western countries such as the United States.

To this end, the UAE continues to be a leader in the GCC, the organization of southern gulf states created in 1981. However, the individual GCC states each have very weak military forces and face their own problems in upgrading their military capabilities. In addition, it has proved difficult politically for the GCC countries to coordinate their military purchases and training in a manner that would produce a unified regional military defense system.

Therefore, most observers agree that the UAE's best defense for the near future will be cooperation with the United States and other Western nations. In recent years, the UAE's leaders have appeared to recognize this need for U.S. help. The UAE has defense treaties with Britain and France, and

THE U.S. MILITARY IN THE UAE

The United States maintains a significant military presence in the UAE that has increased over recent years, making the UAE one of America's most stable and important Middle East allies. Under the terms of the U.S.-UAE defense agreement (the Defense Cooperation Agreement of 1994), for example, the United States has access to a number of military facilities in the UAE. These include Al-Dhafra Air Base, located about an hour outside of Abu Dhabi and staffed by about three hundred U.S. military personnel. Al-Dhafra was used by the U.S. Air Force to conduct refueling missions during the 1990s as part of its monitoring of southern Iraq, and to launch bomber and spy planes during the United States' 2001 operation to oust the Taliban from Afghanistan. Similarly, a base at Fujairah is used as a center for U.S. air cargo shipments. Like Al-Dhafra, it was used by U.S. forces during the Afghanistan war. The U.S. military also depends on the UAE's modern seaports. The port at Jebel Ali in Dubai, in particular, is visited hundreds of times each year by U.S. Navy vessels in the gulf, but other ports such as Port Rashid in Dubai and Port Zayed in Abu Dhabi are also important for U.S. activities. In addition, the United States has built a remote operating base, called the Arkansas Anchorage, eighty miles offshore from the UAE in the Persian Gulf. The access to UAE ports and facilities gives the United States a place from which to stage military operations in the Middle East, and at the same time the U.S. military presence provides the UAE with security and protection.

the UAE and the United States maintain close military cooperation under their 1994 Defense Cooperation Agreement. The two sides conduct joint training exercises and the United States maintains a constant presence in the UAE. Hundreds of U.S. military personnel are stationed at Al-Dhafra, a military air base about an hour from Abu Dhabi, and U.S. Navy vessels frequently use a number of the UAE's ports for shipping cargo to destinations in the Persian Gulf.

Yet UAE leaders realize that the country's alliances with the West must be balanced against a growing anti-American sentiment in the Middle East. News reports suggest that U.S. support for Israel, its stationing of troops in Muslim nations, and its occupation of Iraq, among other actions, have caused many radical Arabs and Muslims to see the United States as an enemy of Arabs. As a moderate Arab nation that is openly friendly with America and other Western nations, therefore, experts say the UAE could in the future become more of a terrorist target.

How the UAE's leaders respond in the future to these challenges, observers agree, will determine whether it will continue to be the stable and prosperous nation it is today.

A U.S. gunboat patrols the waters off Fujairah. The U.S. military maintains a strong presence in the UAE.

FACTS ABOUT THE UNITED ARAB EMIRATES

GEOGRAPHY

Location: Middle East, bordering the Gulf of Oman and the Persian Gulf, between Oman and Saudi Arabia; bordered by Oman, Qatar, and Saudi Arabia

Total area: 32,000 square miles

Comparative area: slightly smaller than the state of Maine

Coastline: 817 miles

Climate: desert, cooler in eastern mountains

Terrain: flat, barren coastal plain merging into rolling sand dunes of vast desert, mountains in east

Natural resources: petroleum, natural gas

Land use: 0.48%, arable land; 0.49%, permanent crops; 99.03%, other (1998 estimate)

Natural hazards: frequent sand and dust storms

Environmental issues: lack of natural freshwater resources compensated by desalination plants; desertification; beach pollution from oil spills

PEOPLE

Population: 2,484,818 (July 2003 estimate), including 1,606,079 non-nationals

Age structure: 26.7%, 0–14 years (male 338,245; female 324,866); 70.4%, 15–64 years (male 1,087,927; female 661,349); 2.9%, 65 years and over (male 52,059; female 20,372) (2003 estimate)

Population growth rate: 1.57% (2003 estimate)

Birth rate: 18.48 births/1,000 population (2003 estimate)

Death rate: 4.02 deaths/1,000 population (2003 estimate)

Infant mortality rate: 15.58 deaths/1,000 live births (2003 estimate)

Life expectancy: 74.75 years; male, 72.28 years; female, 77.35 years (2003 estimate)

Fertility rate: 3.09 children born/woman (2003 estimate)

Ethnic groups: 19%, Emirati; 23%, other Arab and Iranian; 50%, south Asian; 8%, other

Religions: 96%, Muslim (Sunni 84%, Shia 16%); 4%, Christian, Hindu, and other

Languages: Arabic (official), Farsi, English, Hindi, Urdu

Literacy rate (age 15 and over): 77.9%; male, 76.1%; female, 81.7%; (2003 estimate)

GOVERNMENT

Type: federation with specified powers delegated to the UAE federal government and other powers reserved to member emirates

Capital: Abu Dhabi

Administrative divisions: 7 emirates (Abu Dhabi, Dubai, Sharjah, Fujairah, Ras al-Khaimah, Umm al Qaywayn, Ajman)

National holiday: Independence Day, December 2, 1971

Date of independence: December 2, 1971 (from Britain)

Constitution: December 2, 1971 (made permanent 1996)

Executive branch: Chief of State—President (Zayed bin Sultan al-Nuhayyan since December 2, 1971); Vice President (Maktum bin Rashid al-Maktum since October 8, 1990). Head of Government—Prime Minister (Maktum bin Rashid al-Maktum since October 8, 1990); Deputy Prime Minister (Sultan bin Zayid al-Nuhayyan since November 20, 1990). Cabinet—Council of Ministers, appointed by the president.

Legal system: Federal court system introduced in 1971; except for Dubai and Ras al-Khaimah, not all the emirates are fully integrated into the federal system; all emirates have secular and Islamic law for civil, criminal, and high courts.

Political parties: none

Legislative branch: Federal National Council (40 seats, members appointed by the rulers of the constituent states to serve two-year terms), no elections

Judicial branch: Union Supreme Court (judges are appointed by the president)

Flag description: three equal horizontal bands of green (top), white, and black with a wider vertical red band on the hoist side

ECONOMY

Gross domestic product (GDP): $53.97 billion (2002 estimate); real growth, 1.8% (2002 estimate); GDP per capita, $22,100 (2002 estimate); GDP composition—agriculture, 3%; industry, 46%; services, 51% (2000 estimate)

Labor force: 1.6 million; 73.9% of the population in the 15–64 age group is nonnational (July 2002 estimate)

Industries: petroleum, fishing, petrochemicals, construction materials, some boatbuilding, handicrafts, pearling

Agricultural products: dates, vegetables, watermelons, poultry, eggs, dairy products, fish

Exports: $44.9 billion (2002 estimate)

Imports: $30.8 billion (2002 estimate)

Debt: $18.5 billion (2002 estimate)

Economic aid: none

Currency: Emirati dirham (AED)

NOTES

CHAPTER 1: HIDDEN RICHES

1. Rosemarie Said Zahlan, *The Origins of the United Arab Emirates: A Political and Social History of the Trucial States.* London: Macmillan, 1978, p. 2.

2. Malcolm C. Peck, *The United Arab Emirates: A Venture in Unity.* Boulder, CO: Westview Press, 1986, p. 18.

CHAPTER 2: THE JOURNEY TO PROSPERITY

3. Eric Hoogland and Anthony Toth, "United Arab Emirates—Economy," in *Persian Gulf States: Country Studies,* ed. Helen Chapin Metz. Washington, DC: Government Printing Office, 1994, p. 214.

4. Peck, *The United Arab Emirates,* pp. 25–26.

5. Rosemarie Said Zahlan, *The Making of the Modern Gulf States: Kuwait, Bahrain, Qatar, the United Arab Emirates and Oman.* London: Unwin Hyman, 1989, p. 8.

6. Peck, *The United Arab Emirates,* p. 32.

7. Zahlan, *The Making of the Modern Gulf States,* p. 15.

8. Ali Mohammed Khalifa, *The United Arab Emirates: Unity in Fragmentation.* Boulder, CO: Westview Press, 1979, p. 27.

9. Quoted in Peck, *The United Arab Emirates,* 47.

10. Abdullah Omran Taryam, *The Establishment of the United Arab Emirates: 1950–85.* New York: Croom Helm, 1987, p. 77.

11. Quoted in Peck, *The United Arab Emirates,* p. 49.

12. Quoted in Taryam, *The Establishment of the United Arab Emirates,* p. 176.

CHAPTER 3: UNITY AND PROGRESS

13. Quoted in Taryam, *The Establishment of the United Arab Emirates,* p. 201.

14. Hassan Hamdan al-Alkim, *The Foreign Policy of the United Arab Emirates*. London: Saqi Books, 1989, p. 33.

15. Peck, *The United Arab Emirates*, p. 125.

16. al-Alkim, *The Foreign Policy of the United Arab Emirates*, p. 46.

CHAPTER 4: TRADITION, RELIGION, AND CULTURE

17. Frauke Heard-Bey, *From Trucial States to United Arab Emirates*. London: Longman, 1982, p. 405.

18. Khalifa, *The United Arab Emirates*, p. 95.

19. Quoted in Khalifa, *The United Arab Emirates*, p. 100.

20. Peck, *The United Arab Emirates*, p. 61.

21. ArabNet, "Traditional Music in the Emirates," 2002. www.arab.net/uae/ue_music.htm.

CHAPTER 5: LIFE IN THE MODERN UAE

22. Peck, *The United Arab Emirates*, p. 66.

23. Anthony H. Cordesman, *Bahrain, Oman, Qatar, and the UAE: Challenges of Security*. Boulder, CO: Westview Press, 1997, p. 337.

24. Habeeb Salloum, "Women in the United Arab Emirates," *Contemporary Review*, August 2003.

25. Quoted in Salloum, "Women in the United Arab Emirates."

26. Quoted in UAE Interact, "CNN Lauds Freedom, Facilities in Dubai," February 27, 2004. www.uaeinteract.com/news/default.asp?old=27&mm=2&yy=2004&image2.x=41&image2.y=18.

CHAPTER 6: CHALLENGES AHEAD

27. Eesa Mohammed Bastaki, "H.H. Sheikh Zayed bin Sultan Al Nahyan, President of the United Arab Emirates," 2003. http://faculty.uaeu.ac.ae/~eesa/History/zayed.html.

28. Cordesman, *Bahrain, Oman, Qatar, and the UAE*, p. 297.

29. Cordesman, *Bahrain, Oman, Qatar, and the UAE*, p. 337.

30. Quoted in Richard H. Curtiss, "The UAE: From Bold Dream to Spectacular Reality in One Generation," *Washington Report on Middle East Affairs*, December 1995, www.wrmea.com/backissues/1295/9512048.html.

CHRONOLOGY

1600s

A number of different Arab tribes control the southern Persian Gulf area. The Bani Yas tribe rules the desert area now called Abu Dhabi, and a group of tribes known as the Qawasim controlled the northern coastal region.

1622

British and Persian forces capture the island of Hormuz, on the Persian/Iranian side of the gulf, defeating Portugal's hold on the gulf trade route. Thereafter, the British, Dutch, and French compete to control the area.

1700s

Britain becomes the dominant European power in the gulf.

1819

British military forces attack and defeat the Qawasim.

1820

Britain and tribal sheikhs from the southern Persian Gulf sign a treaty, the General Treaty of Peace.

1835

Britain and the sheikhs sign a second treaty; this later becomes the Perpetual Maritime Truce of 1853.

1892

The Treaty of 1892 is signed between the Trucial States and Britain.

1929

A worldwide depression reduces the demand for pearls and the Japanese develop the cultured pearl industry, destroying the Trucial States' pearl market.

1937

Sheikh Saeed, the ruler of Dubai, grants the first oil concession in the Trucial States, quickly followed by concessions in Ras al-Khaimah, Abu Dhabi, and Ajman.

1939

World War II delays the search for oil in the Trucial States.

1959

The first big oil reserve is discovered off the coast of Abu Dhabi, producing significant oil revenues for the sheikhdom by 1963.

1951

A security force called the Trucial Oman Scouts is formed by the British in Sharjah.

1952

The British create the Trucial States Council (TSC), a body with representatives from each of the seven Trucial sheikhdoms.

1960

A large oil reserve is discovered in Dubai. Oil is also soon discovered in Sharjah and Ras al-Khaimah.

1966

August—Sheikh Zayed bin Sultan al-Nuhayyan becomes ruler of Abu Dhabi. Britain sets up the development fund, which is used to finance development throughout the region.

1968

Britain announces it will withdraw from the Persian Gulf by the end of 1971. An agreement is signed to create a federation between Abu Dhabi and Dubai, and other neighboring sheikhs are invited to join. The seven UAE emirates plus two nearby states—Qatar and Bahrain—agree to form a nine-member federation (the Dubai Agreement).

1971

November—Iran occupies the islands of Greater and Lesser Tunb and Abu Musa.

December—the six states of Abu Dhabi, Dubai, Fujairah, Sharjah, Ajman, and Umm al Qaywayn announce their independence from Britain and form a federation called

United Arab Emirates. Sheikh Zayed bin Sultan al-Nuhayyan is elected president of the new country.

The UAE joins the Arab League.

1972

Ras al-Khaimah joins the federation.

The Federal National Council (FNC) is created.

1974

Zayed negotiates an accord to settle a long-standing territorial dispute between the UAE and Saudi Arabia.

1981

The UAE helps found the Gulf Cooperation Council (GCC).

1991

UAE forces join the U.S. coalition against Iraq after the invasion of Kuwait.

1992

Iran reasserts full control over islands belonging to Sharjah and Ras al-Khaimah.

1994

July—The UAE and the United States sign an agreement called the Defense Cooperation Agreement, providing for close military ties between the two countries.

1996

The UAE adopts a permanent constitution.

2003

Sheikh Saqr bin Mohammed al-Qassimi, ruler of Ras al-Khaimah, demotes his eldest son, Sheikh Khalid, and appoints his fourth son, Shaikh Saud, as crown prince, causing street protests. Order is restored after Abu Dhabi sends armored vehicles to put down the uprising.

2003–2004

The UAE cooperates with the United States on rebuilding Iraq after U.S. coalition forces topple Saddam Hussein's regime.

FOR FURTHER READING

BOOKS

Byron Augustin, *United Arab Emirates*. New York: Children's Press, 2002. Describes the UAE's geography, history, and culture.

Julia Johnson, *U.A.E.* New York: Chelsea House, 1987. Provides an overview of the country of the UAE.

Jason Levin, *From the Desert to the Derby: Inside the Ruling Family of Dubai's Billion-Dollar Quest to Win America's Greatest Horse Race*. New York: Daily Racing Form Press, 2002. An entertaining account of Sheikh Mohammed bin Rashid al-Maktoum's (the crown prince of Dubai) quest to win the Kentucky Derby in 2002.

WEB SITES

Government of the United Arab Emirates (www.uae.gov. ae). A general UAE government site providing information about culture, religion, and other topics, and links to many ministries.

UAE, ArabNet (www.arab.net/uae). A Web site run by a Saudi Arabia news service providing information about UAE's history, culture, business, and geography, as well as links to other helpful Web sites.

UAE Interact (www.uaeinteract.com/culture/default.asp). The official site for the Ministry of Information and Culture for the UAE, which provides a wealth of news and information about life in the country.

UAE Pages (www.uae.org.ae). A Web site run by Etisalat, the UAE's government-run communications company. It is a good source of general, social, business, and tourist information.

United Arab Emirates Consular Information Sheet, Bureau of Consular Affairs, U.S. Department of State (http://

travel.state. gov/travel/uae.html). A U.S. government Web site providing information for people who plan to visit the UAE.

The World Factbook 2003; United Arab Emirates, U.S. Central Intelligence Agency (www.cia.gov/cia/publications/ factbook/geos/ae.html). This U.S. government Web site provides geographical, political, economic, and other information on the UAE.

INTERNET SOURCE

Eesa Mohammed Bastaki, "H.H. Sheikh Zayed bin Sultan Al Nahyan, President of the United Arab Emirates," 2003. (http://faculty.uaeu.ac.ae/~eesa/History/zayed.html.)

WORKS CONSULTED

BOOKS

Hassan Hamdan al-Alkim, *The Foreign Policy of the United Arab Emirates*. London: Saqi Books, 1989. A study of the early years of the UAE's foreign policy, including its relations with Saudi Arabia, Iran, and the Palestinians.

Judith Caesar, *Writing Off the Beaten Track: Reflections on the Meaning of Travel and Culture in the Middle East*. Syracuse, NY: Syracuse University Press, 2002. An American visitor's perceptions of life in the UAE.

Anthony H. Cordesman, *Bahrain, Oman, Qatar, and the UAE: Challenges of Security*. Boulder, CO: Westview Press, 1997. An exploration of the stresses on the UAE and a discussion of the challenges facing the country in the future.

Donald Hawley, *The Trucial States*. London: Allen & Unwin, 1970. A history of the Trucial States before they united to become the UAE.

Frauke Heard-Bey, *From Trucial States to United Arab Emirates*. London: Longman, 1982. A political, social, and economic history of the seven individual emirates of the UAE through their first ten years as a federation.

Ali Mohammed Khalifa, *The United Arab Emirates: Unity in Fragmentation*. Boulder, CO: Westview Press, 1979. A scholarly study of the aspects of the UAE that favor and disfavor unity among the emirates.

Helen Chapin Metz, ed., *Persian Gulf States: Country Studies*. Washington, DC: Government Printing Office, 1994. An overview of the geography, history, economy, society, and politics of the UAE and neighboring gulf states.

Malcolm C. Peck, *The United Arab Emirates: A Venture in Unity*. Boulder, CO: Westview Press, 1986. A highly readable discussion of the UAE and its people, covering the areas of geography, history, society and culture, economy, and politics.

Linda Usra Soffan, *The Women of the United Arab Emirates*. Totowa, NJ: Barnes & Noble Books, 1980. A study of the role of women in the UAE, in both their traditional roles as wives and mothers, and in education and work settings.

Abdullah Omran Taryam, *The Establishment of the United Arab Emirates: 1950–85*. New York: Croom Helm, 1987. An examination of the events that led to the creation of the UAE and its early development.

Rosemarie Said Zahlan, *The Making of the Modern Gulf States: Kuwait, Bahrain, Qatar, the United Arab Emirates and Oman*. London: Unwin Hyman, 1989. This book tells the story of the formation of each of the gulf states (the UAE, Kuwait, Bahrain, Qatar, and Oman).

———, *The Origins of the United Arab Emirates: A Political and Social History of the Trucial States*. London: Macmillan, 1978. A detailed account of the origins and early history of the UAE.

PERIODICALS

APS Diplomat Strategic Balance in the Middle East, "UAE— The Campaign Against Terror—Part 18," June 9, 2003.

———, "UAE—Co-operating with the US," June 9, 2003.

———, "UAE—Military Linkages," June 9, 2003.

Ashok Dutta, "Looking Inwards," *Middle East Economic Digest*, October 31, 2003.

Habeeb Salloum, "Women in the United Arab Emirates," *Contemporary Review*, August 2003.

INTERNET SOURCES

Arab Advisors Group, "UAE Internet Revenues Set to Rise," May 15, 2002. www.nua.ie/surveys/index.cgi?f=VS&art _id=905357955&rel=true.

Arabian Horse Association, "Arabian Horse History and Heritage," 2004. www.arabianhorses.org/education/educa tion_ history_intro.asp.

ArabNet, "Traditional Music in the Emirates," 2002. www. arab.net/uae/ue_music.htm.

Elizabeth R. Aston, "A Brief Introduction to the Geology of the United Arab Emirates," Emirates Natural History Group, www.enhg.org/b/b26/26_02.htm.

Eesa Mohammed Bastaki, "H.H. Sheikh Zayed bin Sultan Al Nahyan, President of the United Arab Emirates," 2003. http://faculty. uaeu.ac.ae/~eesa/History/zayed.html.

BBC News, "Timeline: United Arab Emirates," http://news. bbc.co. uk/1/hi/world/middle_east/country_profiles/828687. stm.

Center for the Study of Global Change, "United Arab Emirates," 2001. http://webdb.iu.edu/internationalprograms /scripts/accesscoverpage.cfm?country=united%20arab %20emirates.

Citizenship and Immigration Canada, "Cultural Profiles Project: United Arab Emirates," www.settlement.org/cp/ english/uae.

Richard H. Curtiss, "The UAE: From Bold Dream to Spectacular Reality in One Generation," *Washington Report on Middle East Affairs*, December 1995. www.wrmea.com/ backissues/1295/9512048.html.

Data Dubai, "Beaches," www.datadubai.com/beaches.htm.

———, "Wildlife: Dugongs," www.datadubai.com/dgong.htm.

Emirates, "Date Palms in the UAE," November/December 1983. http://enhg5.4t.com/b/b22/22_26.htm.

The Emirates Network, "Biography of Sheikh Zayed bin Sultan Al Nahyan," 2004. http://guide.theemiratesnetwork. com/ basics/zayed.php.

Energy Information Organization, U.S. Department of Energy, "United Arab Emirates Country Analysis Brief," February 4, 2004. www.eia.doe.gov/emeu/cabs/uae.html.

Exploitz.com, "United Arab Emirates—Ruling Families Summary," January 1993. www.exploitz.com/United-Arab-Emirates-Ruling-Families-Summary-cg.php.

Government of the United Arab Emirates, "Oil and Gas," www.uae.gov.ae/Government/oil_gas.htm.

———, "Women in UAE," www.uae.gov.ae/Government/women.htm.

Human Rights Watch, "United Arab Emirates," *The Internet in the Mideast and North Africa: Free Expression and Censorship*, June 1999. www.hrw.org/advocacy/internet/mena/uae.htm.

International Press Institute, "United Arab Emirates," *2003 World Press Freedom Review*, www.freemedia.at/wpfr/Mena/uae.htm.

Aftab Kazmi, "Camel's Milk More Nutritious than Cow's," *Gulf News*, Jury 20, 2002. www.gulfnews.com/Articles/news.asp?ArticleID=58230.

Yasser Mahgoub, "Architecture in the United Arab Emirates," Fortune City, http://victorian.fortunecity.com/dali/428/uaearch/uaearch6.htm#Architecture.

MSN Encarta, "United Arab Emirates," http://encarta.msn.com/encyclopedia_761560366/United_Arab_Emirates.html.

Sharjah Liaison Office, American University, "Sharjah, United Arab Emirates," October 11, 2000. www.american.edu/sharjah/AUS_Info/Sharjah_Campus/Sharjah_UAE/sharjah_uae.html.

Southeast Asia Tours, "Travel Information—Dubai," http://southtravels.com/middleeast/uae/culture.html.

TEND 2000, "The United Arab Emirates," http://crm.hct.ac.ae/ events/archive/tend/uae.html.

UAE Interact, "The Camel—God's Gift to the Bedouin," www.uaeinteract.com/history/trad/trd07.asp.

———, "CNN Lauds Freedom, Facilities in Dubai," February 27, 2004. www.uaeinteract.com/news/default.asp?01d=27&mm=2&yy=2004&image2.x=41&image2.y=18.

———, "Government—Development Aid," www.uaeinteract.com/government/development_aid.asp.

———, "Government—Foreign Policy," www.uaeinteract.com/govern ment/foreign_policy.asp.

———, "Government—Political System," www.uaeinteract.com/government/political_system.asp.

————, "UAE Sixth Largest Exporter of Dates to Global Markets," April 29, 2004. www.uaeinteract.com/news/default. asp?01d=29&mm=4&yy=2004&image2.x=27&image2.y=17.

————, "United Arab Emirates Culture," 2000. www.uaein teract.com/culture/default.asp.

United Nations Development Programme, "Constitution: United Arab Emirates," www.pogar.org/countries/consti tution.asp?cid=21.

U.S. Department of State, Report on International Religious Freedom, United Arab Emirates, September 9, 1999. Available at Jewish Virtual Library, www.us-israel.org/jsource/ anti-semitism/reluae99.html.

World InfoZone, "United Arab Emirates Information," www. worldinfozone.com/country.php?country=UAE.

Yahoo Travel, "United Arab Emirates Introduction," 2004. http://travel.yahoo.com/p-travelguide-502320-united_arab_ emirates_introduction-i.

INDEX

PICTURE CREDITS

ABOUT THE AUTHOR

Debra A. Miller is a writer and lawyer with an interest in current events and history. She began her law career in Washington, D.C., where she worked on legislative, policy, and legal matters in government, public interest, and private law firm positions. She now lives with her husband in Encinitas, California. She has written and edited publications for legal publishers, as well as numerous books and anthologies on historical and political topics.